The People
Skills Revolution

The People Skills Revolution

A step by step approach to developing sophisticated people skills

PAMELA E. MILNE

GLOBAL
professional
publishing

Global Professional Publishing Ltd
Random Acres
Slip Mill Lane
Hawkhurst
Cranbrook
Kent TN18 5AD
Email: publishing@gppbooks.com

Global Professional Publishing Ltd believes that the sources of information upon which the book is based are reliable, and has made every effort to ensure the complete accuracy of the text. However, neither Global Professional Publishing Ltd, the authors nor any contributors can accept any legal responsibility whatsoever for consequences that may arise from errors or omissions or any opinion or advice given.

ISBN 978-1-906403-72-0

Printed in the United Kingdom by Berforts

With thanks to all those people who developed me while I was busy developing them.

Contents

Acknowledgements

Michael Young and Daybreak Pictures, producers of the film Endgame, for permission to print an extract from an interview with Michael Young broadcast on the Channel 4 website on 25 April 2009.

The Random House Group Ltd for permission to quote from *Great Hatred, Little Room: Making Peace in Northern Ireland* by Jonathan Powell published by the Bodley Head, and for permission to quote from *Making Peace* by George J Mitchell published by William Heinemann.

Introduction

When I established my change consultancy in 1993, I tried to work out what to call my company. After much soul-searching, I realised that what I am about is finding solutions to problems. I am an eternal optimist, who believes that there is always a solution to any difficulty. It might not always be the solution you want, when you want it. It might not even be the one you expect or hope for, but my experience has shown me that there is always a solution. This led me to call my business Solutions Unlimited.

This book is the culmination of over 20 years of helping clients to work out their problems, having dialogues with them and observing patterns. My main achievement during this time has been to develop a model I call the 'Continuum of interpersonal skills' (see Chapter 2 and Annex 1), which combined with a number of innovative approaches and some tried-and-tested techniques, has become a highly predictable road map for developing increasingly complex interpersonal skills in a step-by-step manner.

This model suggests that the concept 'I positive, you positive' underpins all successful interactions between people, and that once people achieve this through becoming more assertive, they can quite naturally progress to influencing, negotiating, conciliation, taking a stand and making peace. In fact, this approach has become so stable and effective that when I get a new client or group, all I have to do is get out my 'toolkit' and get to work.

Before I go on to the interesting and useful ideas contained in this book, I want to tell you something about myself. I have a Master's degree in Change Agent Skills and Strategies from the University of Surrey and a BSc (Economics) from the University of London and have worked extensively in the corporate world and in the public sector as an executive coach, outplacement consultant and management trainer.

For most of my life I have also suffered from chronically low self-esteem, which I put down to being born with a cleft palate and harelip. In fact, it was my negative beliefs system, combined with a lack of interpersonal skills that caused the difficulties I experienced. It was only when I started to improve my interpersonal skills, and see things from a more positive perspective, that I genuinely began to feel more optimistic. I now believe that anyone can become more successful, if they revisit their beliefs and systematically develop their communication skills when dealing with others.

I wrote this book because one of my exceptional long-term clients challenged me to write it as my own development opportunity.

When I asked this client who is a director of finance to write something about his experience of us working together using the continuum of interpersonal skills model this is what he wrote.

Not world peace but a big step along the way!
The people's skills revolution

When I tell people at parties I am a finance director in an NHS Hospital Trust they generally think I am a "boffin" or a technical geek! Often they express deep sympathy with statements like "that must be a very difficult job" or once I was accused of being mad.

By the end of such conversations invariably peoples' opinions have changed. I explain to them it's all about people. Yes, as a finance director in a financially challenged NHS Trust it really is all about people. Yes, systems of financial control, strong governance are essential building blocks, are absolutely essential, but to get an organisation to motor to achieve what could never be dreamed of – people, people, people.

I can't overstate the importance of people skills. I hope some of my own near world peace moments will illustrate the value of people skills in a busy NHS setting:

Financially challenged hospital 1

Consultant doctors have power. In one particular hospital there was a particularly powerful consultant who, by virtue of her excellent clinical standing, her ability to be forceful and sometimes to just be difficult, could thwart positive initiatives that she did not agree with or could not see the value in. The problem was this influence pervaded; she certainly knew the "power of chats". I think, wrongly, many people feared her. The challenge was to get her on board to the need to be more efficient and save money whilst not diminishing patient care. How could I do so?

I appealed to her intellectual side and in some way her desire to control by asking her to be my mentor. Imagine she was the finance director's mentor! I did this with a degree of trepidation. What happened was remarkable:

- *we discovered we had many shared values – like wanting the very best for our patients*
- *she learned (although I suspect she always knew) that financial stability really did contribute to great patient care*
- *all our prejudice about each other got worn away*
- *we had a safe environment to negotiate and find common ground.*

I let certain influential people know what I was doing (as did our doctor!) and it sent a message out. We can work together and she was not the person to be feared so much.

The outcome was that as a minimum she didn't get in the way of many important initiatives to make the hospital more efficient. In fact on many occasions I had an ally. The hospital gained three stars, the highest rating possible under the system at that time (patient care measures and financial performance being some of the key measures under this system). But the big prize was the performance enabled the successful securing of major investment into a whole new modern hospital block. Our patients and local population were the winners.

Financially challenged hospital 2

When I joined a large teaching hospital and in the month of joining we closed the accounts for the previous year with a £23m deficit, I knew we were in deep trouble. No amount of clever accounting, strong business processes or desperate cost cutting was going to resolve this. Many of the external stakeholders had calculated that by blaming the hospital and vilifying the management they could keep there own positions.

The strategy was:

- *meet with external stakeholders and explain that they had an investment in success and tap into the politicians to get them to understand failure meant bad news for all.*
- *galvanize the consultant body internally to foster allies and explain to them that by turning round the organisation they would not be under threat from their competitor colleagues in other teaching hospitals (this created an enormous inner strength which makes any external stakeholder think twice about behaving badly towards their own hospital).*
- *deliver some early results to give credibility to the longer-term plan which tempted the stakeholders to support its delivery.*
- *set clear values by which we dealt with internal bad behavior and external bad behavior, in effect developing the first shoots of corporate assertiveness.*

The outcome was a remarkable turnaround in the finances and patient care improvements. We wiped out the deficit in three years.

Contained in these pages are the strategies and approaches that I have worked out in conversation with my clients to resolve many of the issues that they were confronted with. I suspect they may also be similar to the issues you may be faced with in your working and personal life. They have worked for me and they have worked for them. If you internalise the ideas and move out of your 'comfort zone' to try some different techniques and strategies, they will work for you too.

The skills you learn will also continue to develop as you progress through your career. I once coached a service director who had rejected the last coach by turning her back on him and refusing to engage in the process. When I took over she was very fragile and the slightest bit of probing led to tears welling up in her eyes. I worked with her closely over the year long coaching programme and using the approaches contained in this book she became increasingly sophisticated in her use of interpersonal skills and could make the changes in the service provision that she needed to make.

For logistical reasons, the last session was postponed for about 3 months. We then agreed to meet in a restaurant to have lunch and celebrate our work together. I got there first and was waiting for her when this amazingly confident woman wafted into the room and sat down. I hardly recognised her since she had changed so much in the way she talked and the way she carried herself. I sat there mesmorised by the difference in her.

On my way back to the car I bumped into a client I had coached the previous year and commented on the change I had seen in this service director. He worked closely with her and agreed that the change in her had been quite remarkable and said 'and I think there is a lot more where that's come from'.

Once you start to believe that change is possible, start to develop the skills in the book and start to achieve impressive results, you will continually look for opportunities to use and develop your skills. Life starts to become a playground rather than a battle field and things that previously seemed impossible become possible.

A note on how to read this book.

I would suggest that you read the book all the way through to get a sense of the flow of the story, and then go back and consider the ideas presented in each chapter in the light of your experiences. Alternatively, you can integrate your own ideas and thoughts as you go along. Whichever way you read the book, it is important to remember that the skills I describe are incremental and you need to practise the earlier skills before you can master the later ones.

I believe it takes about a year to move from assertiveness or influencing to negotiation or conciliation. So take your time to absorb the information, and integrate the skills and gain the benefits that are available at whichever level you are working on, before progressing to the next set of skills.

Looking at your behaviour differently can be challenging and tiring. So pace yourself as you read the book. Start at the beginning of the continuum even if you feel a resistance to do this. I believe that nearly all interpersonal skills difficulties are brought about by negative thinking and a lack of assertiveness so be open minded to looking at issues and people differently. I would suggest that you do not go onto another skill until you have achieved success in the one you have just tried. This book is based on the idea that success breeds success so you undermine this process if you jump from one skill to another without integrating your learning.

As you read this book highlight or make a note on the points that struck you the most.

One client highlighted the sentence

> *'Then there is a much smaller group of people who are loved and respected, believe in themselves and others, achieve their goals fairly and directly, do not dwell on the past and work towards solutions for the common good.'*

She went on to tell me that it was her goal to be one of those people. So set your aims high when reading this book and start to believe that you can achieve them.

Read the text slowly so you can integrate your learning as you go. I highly recommend that you complete the reactionnaires at the end of the skills-based chapters in order to bring your experience of reading the book to life and enable you to apply the ideas and concepts to your own business environment. They will also prompt you to take action since the only way to gain skills is to step out of your comfort zone and try the techniques. Even if it feels a bit messy at the beginning, keep going until the skills become part of your normal behaviour.

I hope you find the journey as fascinating as I have.

Chapter 1

The Wisdom of Patterns

Sometimes, relating to people can feel very random. What works for one person fails miserably for someone else when you try out the same approach with them.

When working with clients to resolve their issues, I realised that most people's questions when dealing with others are exactly the same as everybody else's. Most of us just do not realise this. The continuum of interpersonal skills that I developed (see Annex 2) evolved gradually, when I was helping my clients to work out some practical solutions to what turned out to be some very common problems.

From my experience there are three types of people in the world. There are those who pursue their goals relentlessly with no concern for others. There are many more who wish they could achieve their goals but feel they cannot. Then there is a much smaller group of people who are loved and respected, believe in themselves and others, achieve their goals fairly and directly, do not dwell on the past and work towards solutions for the common good.

While it is tempting to look at these exceptional people and assume that these skills were innate these charming and confident people were not born that way. They are simply displaying a set of acquired skills and behaviours, which almost anyone with a degree of intelligence, application and an open mind can learn.

This book will help you to move from the group who wish they could achieve their goals but feel they cannot, into the group who feel they can achieve their goals fairly and directly. In the process, you will also find that people want to be around you and to help you to achieve your goals.

If you are one of those people who pursue their goals relentlessly with no concern for others, it will also help you. It will enable you to understand people more, become more people-focused and decide whether you want to continue to put your needs above the needs of others. Although this is a more difficult transition, the ideas in the book will assist you if you genuinely want to change your behaviour, to live and work in a more relaxed and peaceful environment.

Throughout my career as an executive coach and management consultant I have been in the privileged position of working with some remarkable people, sometimes over a long period of time. About ten years ago I started coaching a director of finance, who was very skilled interpersonally. Many of our chats were about strategy and how to influence at a very senior – and sometimes national – level. When he changed roles, as he did quite frequently, I moved with him and he increasingly referred me to his colleagues and his mentees, who then recommended me to their colleagues. In this way I gained a great deal of experience in working with finance directors and other board-level directors.

While working with these clients and training other staff, I began to notice a pattern in the way that people developed, which I called the 'continuum of interpersonal skills'. This is based on a very simple idea that assertiveness underpins all effective communication and that once people have achieved this, they very naturally and rapidly progress to the skills of influencing, negotiation, conciliation, taking a stand and making peace. Of course, not everyone will consistently improve their skills to become a peacemaker – most of us might not want to or even get the opportunity, but given the right tools, they can significantly and positively change the impact they have on people.

Since identifying the model, I have used it quite deliberately to develop the people I coach and train. More often than not I have found that if I explain a concept or an approach to a client, it leads to a change of behaviour and the achievement of much more effective outcomes. As a result, I am able to pinpoint their issues very quickly and effectively and give them the tools they need to become increasingly more effective when working with others.

The results have been quite remarkable. Not only does the improvement in skills impact on them but also on their staff and the wider organisation. It makes the development process much more predictable, since the client effectively knows where they are heading when they are working through the process. As they see the improvement in themselves, the positive slant to the model makes them believe, quite rightly, that the exceptional skills they see others using are within their reach.

I then began to wonder if I simply explained in writing what I explain directly to my clients, in a step-by-step 'pull different levers, push different buttons' way, whether the effect would be the same? Having shared this book with a number of early readers, I believe this to be the case.

It is not rocket science. In fact, when you read this book, you may think that some of the techniques are incredibly simple and logical. They have an innate wisdom to them, which makes people think that at some level they knew them already. If you try them out, you will find that they work for you too and you should start to make rapid progress towards achieving your goals.

The continuum of interpersonal skills is based on the idea that you need some basic underpinning human interaction skills before you can start to get your needs met directly and honestly. So although you may have picked up this book to learn how to negotiate world peace and you want to just flick to those pages, I can honestly tell you that you will be wasting your time if you do not have the basic underlying skills which support the more advanced ones.

As I lead you through the process, you will be amazed at the different results you start to achieve. This in turn will spur you on to try out some more new skills and your progress will start to become rapid. So slowing down a bit in the beginning is not a waste of time. See it more as laying the foundations; once you have the foundations in place, the rest of the build is easy.

When working with clients, often with very sophisticated interpersonal skills, I discovered that if they hit a problem, somewhere along the line, the problem would be with the underpinning skills. So, if you are going along smoothly and achieving the results that you want to achieve and then hit a block, revisit the more basic skills – you will find your answer there.

I was recently asked: 'Are you really this optimistic or are you just naive?'. Although I might sound naive, using these skills has made me feel incredibly positive about my ability and the ability of others to achieve our goals in a way that benefits everybody.

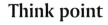

Think point

How would you assess your people skills at the moment?

What effect do your people skills have on your work, home and personal life

What would you like to be able to do differently?

What goals would you like to achieve in your life?

In six months' time?

In one year's time?

In ten years' time?

In your lifetime?

What stops you from achieving these goals?

Chapter 2

The Continuum of Interpersonal Skills

Once I had developed the continuum of interpersonal skills (see Figure 1), I realised that it was a powerful tool to help people to work out where they were now, where they would like to be in the future and how to get there. I have been using it deliberately and consistently to develop clients since 2000. This book will act as a fast track to these higher interpersonal skills and will see you getting better results within weeks – and significantly different outcomes within one year.

Figure 2.1: The continuum of interpersonal skills

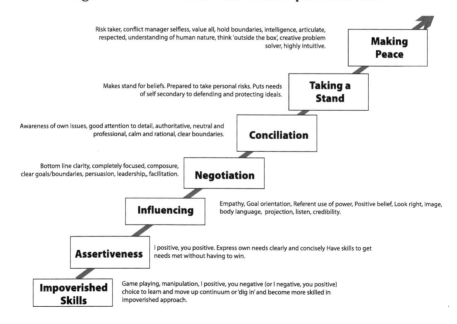

Risk taker, conflict manager selfless, value all, hold boundaries, intelligence, articulate, respected, understanding of human nature, think 'outside the box', creative problem solver, highly intuitive.

Making Peace

Makes stand for beliefs. Prepared to take personal risks. Puts needs of self secondary to defending and protecting ideals.

Taking a Stand

Awareness of own issues, good attention to detail, authoritative, neutral and professional, calm and rational, clear boundaries.

Conciliation

Bottom line clarity, completely focused, composure, clear goals/boundaries, persuasion, leadership,, facilitation.

Negotiation

Influencing

Empathy, Goal orientation, Referent use of power, Positive belief, Look right, image, body language, projection, listen, credibility.

Assertiveness

I positive, you positive. Express own needs clearly and concisely Have skills to get needs met without having to win.

Impoverished Skills

Game playing, manipulation, I positive, you negative (or I negative, you positive) choice to learn and move up continuum or 'dig in' and become more skilled in impoverished approach.

This is how the model evolved. In my first role in people development, I went on an assertiveness course in order to teach a similar programme in my own organisation. Before attending this course I did not actually think that I lacked assertiveness, but by the middle of the programme I realised that I had many more 'issues' than I imagined.

Looking back, learning the techniques of assertiveness laid the foundations for the incremental skill-building change process that I set out in this book. Since that time, I have run hundreds of assertiveness programmes and it still remains my favourite course. This is because you see 'light bulb' moments happen before your eyes.

Assertiveness is the set of skills that makes people feel better about themselves, makes them feel that they can have control of their lives and makes them feel more optimistic about the future. Once people believe that positive change is possible, they then look for the next change that they can try to achieve better results. Attending an assertiveness course tends to be the event that starts this process for many people. For others, it may be the gradual realisation that what they are doing is not working.

After I became more assertive, I started to enjoy life more and as a result started to get better results when working with people. Almost without realising, I began influencing people. I then started to notice the same pattern in the many hundreds of people I worked with during coaching sessions and on courses. As they started to improve and get different outcomes, they tended to make rapid progress, regardless of whether they received further assistance. This made me realise that there was a natural momentum from assertiveness onto the next level of skills.

Achieving a success that you never before thought possible whets your appetite for more skills. The more skills I developed, the more I was able to achieve and the more I wanted to learn new skills. It was not long before I found myself combining my assertiveness and influencing skills to negotiate deals. This turned out to be so profitable and enjoyable that I found myself negotiating virtually everything – from work and industrial contracts to a new house or car.

When working with hundreds of my clients I also noticed a similar tendency. Once people learnt assertiveness skills, they seemed to make rapid progress as they identified and then developed the next level of skills. This got me interested in the idea that interpersonal skills are incremental and that there is a logical build, as people become increasingly more effective in their interactions with others.

From this, I concluded that the interpersonal skill set is stable, predictable, cumulative and can be learnt by anyone, providing they believe that they can get different outcomes and are prepared to step out of their comfort zones to achieve increasingly challenging goals. Put simply, success breeds success.

As people developed their skills in a systematic way, they were becoming increasingly capable of negotiating outcomes that they loved telling me about. They often explained how they had spotted opportunities, influenced people, anticipated events, had almost magical strokes of luck and were able to achieve deals, while others looked on with awe.

Then I started to notice something interesting in my executive coaching clients, who are mostly directors of finance. They knew that they could win in almost any negotiation they entered into. They knew that they could beat the other party and they were choosing not to do so. Instead, they were developing their colleagues and representatives from other organisations that they came into contact with. This could take the form of meetings to identify and work with their concerns, or discussions to share perspectives and provide information that the other party might find useful. Although this was a small group of people, it happened often enough for me to start seeing it as a predictable and natural progression through the stages of interpersonal skills development.

At this point I started to formalise the idea that there was a natural progression through the skills – from assertiveness, through to influencing, negotiation and conciliation – and to use this as a diagnostic tool for my clients. Using this approach, I could assess the current skill set of clients, then predict where they were on the continuum and diagnose what problems they might have in their interactions with others. Sharing this information with them, I found they connected with the concepts I was explaining and could quickly act on the skill development I suggested, to move up to the next level. They were also able to use the continuum to create a common language and to develop the staff working for them. In this way they started to build around them a much more creative, enjoyable and productive environment, which was based on cumulative interpersonal skills acquisition.

Another major influence in developing the continuum of interpersonal skills was reading Nelson Mandela's book the *Long Walk to Freedom*[1]. For a while I had links with Cape Town in South Africa and after visiting Robben Island I was struck by how Nelson Mandela's attitude to life and interpersonal skills has evolved throughout his life. Having spent 27 years in prison, he was able to emerge as a conciliator and a peace maker, having clearly moved through the stages of assertiveness, influencing and conciliation. So although I was believed that at the top of the continuum was the desire to achieve peace I was convinced that there was a step between conciliation and making peace.

Now, working with a very small sample of clients, maybe only three or four who were operating at a very senior level both inside and outside their

---

1   Abacus 2002

organisations, I noticed another potential pattern: they all had tendency to have at least one experience which challenged their values and made them consider what they stood for. As a result, some moved on from their current situation, which they found untenable, while others stood firm on a matter of principle. This process too appeared to be predictable, so I added 'taking a stand' to the continuum of interpersonal skills.

I then became curious to find out if there were any levels beyond taking a stand for what you believe in. The last piece of the puzzle came when reading about exceptional people who made an impact on their societies. These included Michael Young, who helped to broker the peaceful transition to black majority rule in South Africa, and George J Mitchell and Jonathan Powell, who assisted in the Northern Ireland peace process.

As well as being prepared to commit and sometimes risk their lives for what they believed in, they also demonstrated highly developed interpersonal skills to promote inclusive communities. So I have included a stage called 'making peace' on the continuum and talk in Chapter 10 about the skills and beliefs required to operate successfully at this level.

The aspect I most like about the model is that it suggests that everyone can develop their skills to improve their results. It is not magic; it is not accident of birth; it is just simple skills that with a bit of application, patience and good intention most people can learn.

In my work I offer clients new perspectives based on this continuum and am constantly amazed how greater awareness, different outlooks and step-by-step strategies, explained clearly and concisely, seem to be enough for them to make significant and lasting changes in their lives. These suggestions to improve interactions with others are shared in this book. I believe that if you follow them, they will have the same impact on you.

As you follow the suggestions in this book, you will begin to feel more confident and more in control as you change your behaviour. As you change and get better outcomes, you will expect others to notice that you are behaving differently. It can be a bit disappointing when they do not. Be patient. When working with clients who did 360-degree feedback at the start, middle and end of a year-long coaching programme, it was clear that it took at least six months for the people giving the feedback to change their perceptions about the person being coached. This made me realise that although other people may pick up change at a very subtle level, it takes much longer to creep into their awareness and for their perceptions to adjust to the idea that you have changed your behaviour.

Another reaction you may have to the model is to look at it and think, 'So what?'. I have learnt that this is a natural reaction too. When first working with a coaching client, I tend to show them the model at either our first or second meeting, because I think it helps them to understand what I will be focusing on. It also helps them to appreciate that if I start talking about improving assertiveness, which they might consider to be a fairly low-level skill, that I am only doing this in order to facilitate rapid progress up the continuum later. A number of clients have told me that when they first saw the model, they did not quite 'get' what I was trying to say, but that as we began to consciously move up the continuum of interpersonal skills, it started to make complete sense and made them believe that achieving exceptional interpersonal skills was both achievable and predictable.

A chief financial officer's feedback on using The Continuum of Interpersonal Skills

I started working with Pamela on The Continuum of Interpersonal Skills *model before I secured my first board level post. I quickly came to understand that the behaviours and responses I considered to indicate assertiveness on my part where in fact indicators of a lack of, or impoverished, assertiveness skills.*

The most important of its many contributions to my developing skills as a director have been the extent to which work with it has helped me to remain calm and increase my self confidence. This has been fundamental to how I have been able to navigate the most challenging issues so far. Understanding how low key visibility leads to greater comfort in different situations and conversely makes you appear more visible.

Politics, manipulation and game playing can create a stressful environment especially for a newly appointed board member. The Continuum of Interpersonal Skills *model provides insight into the motivating factors that are often behind these behaviours and teaches you how to spot this when it is happening around you and to deal with it in a way that makes you comfortable in these shark infested waters, and in fact to prosper as a result. Working systematically with Pamela through her model has been material to my progress and the success I have achieved in the last two years, and it is central to my plans for the future.*

For one particular client, a community midwife, I did not introduce the concepts at all for three sessions whilst I built her trust in me and reassured her that the process would be helpful to her rather than damaging. It is only when she felt that my intention was honourable and I engaged with her on an emotional level that she was prepared to accept working with me. I gave her an early draft of this book to read as an experiment. I wanted to know what impact, if any, it would have on her.

Six months after we had stopped working together I asked her for feedback. This is what she wrote.

I found The People Skills Revolution *an inspiration to me; it opened my eyes on issues I used to take for granted. For instance, it taught me assertiveness, although I had thought I was assertive; it explained to me the role and the dangers of negative beliefs, making me realise that negative beliefs brought negative thoughts that affected my behaviour. Negative thinking is destructive and infectious but working with this book helped me realise that I could change.*

Pamela's work is a must have for any individual, as it will teach you self awareness skills, influencing skills and how to build rapport. There are different types of people and you can influence all of them in different ways. I got to know what type I was and what type my colleagues were.

I am a person who likes to mind my own business but working with Pamela and her book taught me the power of chats which I had never liked before, not realising how I was missing out on building relationships.

If you want to become a good listener this approach is for you. I have now developed my listening skills and have learnt to love the void. I am now good at negotiation and don't give up anything without getting something in return. I have become an expert at positive beliefs and will never return to being negative again.

I keep going back to the book and its ideas once or twice a week. I feel more confident in myself and in control of my behaviour. When I first looked at the Continuum of Interpersonal Skills model, I thought "I know all of that already". When I started following it step by step, I had to change my beliefs. Now it is difficult for other people to manipulate or bully me.

I used to be very good at "collecting stamps and cashing them in" but now I act on each incident as it happens. My interaction with other people has improved a lot but I also use my skills to build my students and colleagues. Now I am good at 'fogging' whereas before I used to react by defending myself.

At last I have realised and accepted that success breeds success. I have developed insights and skills into building rapport, listening and questioning and communication styles.

I am still amazed. I have learnt how to establish credibility and how to make a request, become aware of the concepts of power, and of the hierarchy of language, a good tool for building rapport. I used to think working hard would get me recognised and I was shocked to learn how people get recognised. Pamela,

The Continuum of Interpersonal Skills *and her* The People Skills Revolution *have equipped me with management skills.*

Chapter 3

The Beliefs and Skills Approach

When learning new skills, two factors play a part: one is clearly learning the skills to achieve different goals; the other is believing that it is possible to achieve different outcomes.

If you have a negative belief, however many skills you learn you will get a negative outcome. If you have a positive belief and a negative set of skills, you will also achieve a negative outcome (if you don't believe me, think of the talent show auditions). The only way to achieve positive change is to have a positive belief that something is possible, backed up by the skills to make this happen. This book works at both levels.

If you are reading this and feeling a bit doubtful, or it conjures up images of people you do not want to be like, the chances are that you might be feeling some resistance to what I am saying.

I know you may have this resistance because I have seen it so many times when I have worked with people. If you are not careful, your preconceptions may undermine your ability to learn new skills. With one client I spent two hours in a coaching session trying to persuade her that it was beneficial to learn influencing skills, but every time I said the word 'influencing', she heard the word 'manipulation'. She was French and said, 'This is me, I can't change the way I am'. But the next time we met she had gone back to France and found a book which talked about how to influence with integrity. Now she was much more amenable to the idea of learning how to influence. She had found a way to make learning the new skills acceptable to her. She then rapidly and happily started to use the skills I shared with her to influence colleagues, friends and family to achieve outcomes that before she had not thought possible.

Her concern does, however, raise an important issue. The skills you will learn to assert yourself, influence and negotiate can be used to manipulate – the main difference comes in your intention. If you intend to manipulate, people on the receiving end will feel used and will feel uncomfortable around you. If you learn to influence them, they will enjoy working with you and will want to contribute to your goals.

The role of negative beliefs

Before starting on the continuum of interpersonal skills and the skills involved at each level, I want to talk about the role played by positive beliefs in achieving goals.

When working with people over the years, I realised that helping people to become more effective was not just about teaching them new skills. Belief systems play a central role. People will not develop new skills if they do not believe they will work or, more importantly, do not believe that they will work for **them**.

When I first started working with people on assertiveness courses, I noticed a layer of negativity in the people I was working with. My first reaction was to think that this goes with the territory on courses like that. Then I began to notice the same pattern on management courses and then in senior executives who I was coaching. This made me wonder whether there was a layer of low self-esteem pervading our society. I think that might be likely. Since we do not talk about things like lack of confidence in work and social circles, there can be a tendency to believe that we are the only person who experiences this.

Contrary to what you might think, negative thinking is not inevitable and it can be changed. We are not born with beliefs – negative or positive. They emerge over time and depend on where we decide to focus our attention. If you do not believe me, think of football supporters. No one is born believing a team is worthy of support. During the process of socialisation, people make a decision to support a particular team by finding something special about them. This might be that they are top of the league, or for less successful teams their support might come from a type of moral superiority, for example that it takes courage to support them. Then they gather all the evidence to support their belief that their team is better than the rest. They can do this even though there may be a substantial amount of evidence to demonstrate that they may not be a particularly high-performing or 'special' team.

To take this one step further, take two successful teams – for example Manchester United and Arsenal – and put a supporter of each team in a room with some football facts and statistics and ask one to convince the other that theirs is the better team. Believe me, it is not going to happen. Once we have identified our beliefs, the only evidence we tend to allow into our thought process is the evidence that supports our belief. This process also operates for the negative or positive thought patterns we have about ourselves.

I also have a theory that the extent of a person's negative beliefs is in direct proportion to the amount of skills, talents and abilities they are suppressing. Now this does sound a bit peculiar, but I think that sometimes it is not possible to celebrate our potential when we are younger. We may get told 'Don't get too big for your boots' or 'I know best' or 'Who do you think you are?'. So we learn to take on the criticism of others and then once our critics are not around we take over the job from them. If a person is particularly bright or talented, it can take a great deal of criticism from ourselves and others to keep that enormous well of possibilities in its place.

As the layers of negativity are peeled back, the blocks on this power are removed and true creativity and capability can be revealed.

I used to live in a very negative world. Because it was my usual thought process, I did not realise that there was another way of thinking. I was lucky that a simple technique that was given to me by a mentor changed my life. He spotted my negativity and knew that it could be changed. Gradually and consistently I used the approach he showed me, to reverse the energy-sapping and obsessive thoughts that handicapped my performance and never allowed me to celebrate my success.

The model my mentor showed me, which helped to clear out my negativity, is set out below.

The cycle of negative beliefs

Put simply, it says that we start off with a negative belief about ourselves and our ability to interact with another person or other people. This negative belief leads to an internal negative reaction, which leads to a performance interruption when we are with the other party, which leads to a confirmation and reinforcement of the original negative belief. Next time we are faced with a similar situation, our negative belief has become even more entrenched. In response, our negative internal reaction will get stronger and we will perform worse than we did before.

In this way, an inkling of a negative thought can become self-reinforcing, until an initial (maybe passing) negative thought can become a firmly held belief. I have mentioned already that when I was younger I had low self-esteem, which I attributed to having a birth defect. This meant that when I approached situations, I felt negative about myself, became very inward-looking and intense. When approached by others, I was very hard work and I was difficult to get to know. The more situations I went into, the worse I felt. Although trying hard with my words, I am sure my body language screamed out my negativity. In the end, I tended to avoid situations where I would feel uncomfortable. Over time, my ability to connect with people seemed to deteriorate rather than improve. So in addition to the 'I think I am unattractive' belief, I also started to acquire beliefs that 'I can't form relationships with people' and 'People don't like me'. In this way, one negative belief sparked off others. Once you get into this negative downward spiral, it is very difficult to get out of it. Negative beliefs can become like matted balls of string, with one negative belief attached to and piggybacking on another.

It is only now that I do not carry these negative beliefs around in my head that I realise how energy-sapping, self-absorbed and destructive they were. Negative beliefs are more common than you might imagine, but most of us do not talk about them openly, so you think it must just be you. I have assisted many highly successful people – from directors to consultants and entrepreneurs – to break the downward spiral of negative thinking and to become much more successful in their work and personal lives. If you have a tendency to live inside your head and worry about what others think of you and constantly have performance anxiety, this approach should help you too.

Here is the basic model that my mentor showed me.

Figure 3.1: The cycle of negative beliefs

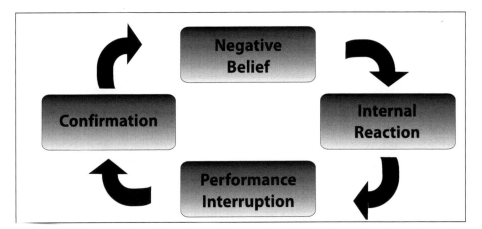

What this model demonstrates is that we can start off with a negative belief, for instance 'I feel invisible'.

This leads to you thinking about things in your head before you have met other people (internal reaction).

Bear in mind that if you have a negative belief about a situation, you will have negative thoughts about the outcome of a meeting – regardless of what the other person thinks about you and the behaviour that they might display to you.

From this belief that 'I feel invisible', some typical internal reactions might be as follows.

- It will be a waste of time.
- I will look like completely stupid **again**.
- They think that I am an idiot.
- I look like a complete pillock not saying anything.
- They always look straight past me.
- What's the point of getting ready, when they will not notice me anyway.
- I will just be looking at everyone else enjoying themselves.

Notice that when you are doing this, you are not creating these internal reactions. You are simply making unconscious thoughts conscious. When you do this exercise, it can be quite shocking to realise that you think these kinds of thoughts about yourself

If you have these thoughts about yourself and then you do go into an interaction with another person, it is no wonder that you start to focus on the thoughts in your head rather than on the person in front of you or on the telephone. Part of you will be engaged in the meeting; the other part of you will be engaged with the thoughts in your head, looking for the evidence to reinforce your negative belief that you think you are invisible.

So instead of paying attention to any positive clues that the other person might be giving out to you in their behaviour, you will focus on when they looked away from you, when they looked bored or impatient or looked at their watch. The thoughts in your head will then say: 'See, they are not noticing me'; 'They think you are wasting their time'; 'They clearly want to get on with seeing the more interesting people'. The proportion of your mental energy is increasingly taken up with listening to your mind's observations on how you are doing, rather than actually engaging with the person (performance interruption).

As you have observed your poor performance, you will walk out of the meeting and reinforce the negative belief that you are invisible by saying: 'See, I was only in there for 5 minutes, during which time she looked at her watch twice, looked irritated and clearly wanted me to leave' (confirmation).

This selective observation will of course reinforce and confirm the belief that you are invisible, meaning that the next time you go around the cycle you will believe it more, until one day you may believe it completely. You will also find that if you go through a few cycles of this negative cycle that your performance will get worse rather than better, and over time you may focus more and more on all the negative elements that you are looking for.

At this point you may decide that it is better to withdraw completely from interactions, rather than experiencing the discomfort of feeling invisible. In the process you will probably create another negative belief: that people do not want you around. You can see from this example how negative beliefs are destructive, self-reinforcing, and generate new, unhelpful beliefs for you to focus on. Negative thinking is habitual thinking and it is infectious.

Try it yourself. Imagine you have a negative belief about yourself – most people have them. Here are some common examples for you to pick from, if you cannot think of any of your own.

- They think I am not good enough.
- Whatever I do or say, it does not make any difference.
- People don't like me.
- People don't listen to me.

The cycle of positive beliefs

The really great thing about the belief cycle approach is that in the same way that it took a long time for your negative beliefs to become entrenched by going around the cycles a few times, you can reverse the process by choosing an alternative positive belief – you do not even have to believe it. Then you just have to be open-minded about the possibility of thinking this new belief. Automatically your brain will start to look for evidence to support the more positive belief and once it finds it, it will keep looking for more. After a few rotations around the cycle, an inkling of a positive belief will gradually start turning in to an actual positive belief.

Figure 3.2: The cycle of positive beliefs

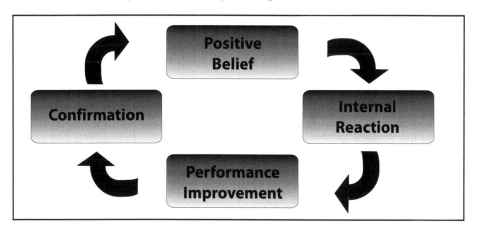

If you do want to change a belief that is not working for you – you can decide to focus your attention elsewhere.

For example, looking at the 'I am invisible' belief. If you just believed that people notice you, your internal reaction would say: 'Well, if people are going to notice me, I had better make myself a bit more presentable. I will buy that new jacket I saw that I thought would be a waste of money. I had better have something to say if people are going to notice me. Since I will not feel so defeated, I will come across a bit more confident in the way I look, stand, speak and sit.'

With this possibility of thinking differently, when you meet people you will pay more attention to them noticing your new presentation, you will notice looks of interest in what you are saying, you will notice when they smile. Things change slowly – they will not all be perfect straight away, but you will start to observe and focus on positive behaviours that you did not see before. Then when you walk away this time, you will say: 'Well, there is still room for improvement, but my performance is getting better'. Each time around the cycle you will experience a positive shift, until one day you will just know that you are visible and that people notice you. This more positive outcome will start you generating some additional positive beliefs about yourself.

Let me show you how the negative and positive belief cycle works with a real example of a coaching conversation that I had with a friend of mine.

> He believed: 'What's the point of trying, when I am just to be tolerated initially and then rejected?'

By the way, he has been a friend of mine for a very long time and I see him as a very sociable, intelligent and upbeat person, so I was very surprised that he held this belief about himself.

I asked him what his internal reactions were in relation to this belief. These were his thoughts.

- They are going to find out what I am like.
- I don't like or respect myself.
- I don't believe I am a strong, worthwhile person to be admired.
- I will eventually be rejected.
- I know what I do is to push them away.
- Whatever I do, they won't like me.
- It's not worth trying.
- I always end up in the same place.
- Once they know me, they won't like me.
- They will see that I am a fraud and a liar.
- I play a game to make them like me.
- I can't show myself, because I haven't got anything that they would want.

As you can imagine, these thoughts led to massive anxiety or performance interruptions when he did meet someone. Because of the complete absorption with his own thoughts, the performance interruption would occur – whoever the person, whatever behaviour they displayed and whatever their intentions towards him.

I then asked him how these internal negative thoughts affected him when he did actually meet someone. He told me that this is how he tended to behave:

- I stare at them.
- I am not brave enough to speak.
- When they speak to me, I try to become what they are looking for.
- I am not real around them.
- I come across more as a clown or tough guy than connecting with the person.
- I don't show the real me.
- I show the bad side of me, so that they will reject me and get it over with.
- I go to extremes – dominant or submissive.
- I can't talk to them.
- I try to be what they want me to be, so I don't get rejected.
- I am nervous and looking for clues that they don't like me.

- I hope that they will hook on to my accent or appearance.
- I am a chameleon. I try out different ways to be.
- I am frightened they are going to see the real me and hurt me.
- I tell them all the bad things.
- I observe myself doing this and think: 'Oh you are doing it again'.
- I react against the impression that you think I am a tough guy.

All this was going on in his head while he was meeting the person, which shows how little mental energy and capacity were left for a genuine interaction, regardless of what their behaviour or level of interest might have been.

As you can imagine, meetings do not go well for him. When he walks away, he thinks the following things, by way of negative confirmation.

- They are not interested.
- They don't know me.
- I am a fraud.
- I have never been appreciated for me because I am too frightened.

This just acts as a confirmation and reinforcement of the belief 'What's the point of trying, when I am just to be tolerated initially and then rejected?'.

I would like to thank my friend for sharing this with me and for being prepared to share it with you. What it shows is a way of negative thinking that is more common in our society than most people realise. Before you can become more confident, the first thing to tackle is the negative thought processes you have within yourself, which adversely impact on your behaviour.

The good news is that starting to change your negative belief system is straightforward. All you need to do is to select a more positive belief that addresses your particular issue – just make sure that you do not include any negative words in the statement.

When I introduced the positive belief cycle with my friend, it went something like this:

'People will accept me because I am good enough.'

This led to the following internal reactions.

- I will feel strong because the basis of any relationship will be built on truth.
- Once people get to know me, they will like me.

- I can show the real me.
- I can accept people liking me.
- I will be happy knowing that I like myself.
- I will be authentic.

Immediately he felt more positive, even though nothing had changed apart from his thought process. When meeting new people, he imagined that he would experience a performance improvement and would feel more confident and be able to:

- say what I want and need, because I will feel accepted by them
- not be worried that when I say what I want they will find me out
- show the real me from the beginning
- feel safe to express what I want and need
- be consistent about my needs
- be more relaxed, confident and stable
- be myself
- face it, if challenged
- feel I have been set free
- be free to express myself as I want
- have a more two-way interaction
- be more interested in them as a person.

As you can see, this is much more a two-way engagement with the other person and less of a dialogue with himself in his brain with another party present. He imagined that if he had experienced the more positive interaction described above, that this would have reinforced and confirmed his emerging new belief that 'people would accept him as he is because he is good enough'. More specifically, he thought that having these kinds of experiences would encourage him in the future to be:

- out more and talk to more people, to see what happens
- more productive
- confident that he can talk to people
- more ready to explore relationships
- ready to regard the world as a great place filled with potential rather than heartache.

The interesting thing about using this model is that nothing needs to change externally for the change to start happening internally. This model breaks cycles of habitual negative thinking – and that is the first thing to tackle, before you start to learn the other interpersonal skills described in this book.

When I shared this model with one of my clients, he told me that the process of looking at negative beliefs had slowed down his thoughts and introduced an increased level of observation. In other words, he became an observer to his thoughts rather than enmeshed in them.

If when you read this, however, you feel you do not have any negative beliefs about yourself – people like this are quite rare, but they do exist – do not go looking for them. Instead, accept your good fortune and concentrate on the skills part of the book. Whether or not you are affected by negative beliefs in the way I have described, it can still be useful to know that other people may suffer from negative beliefs, which may affect how they interact with you. You are then better equipped to understand why people may experience potentially paralysing performance interruptions in your presence.

It is only when I have identified and addressed any negative beliefs that may act as blocks to progress that I will start the skill-building with my clients. This is how one client, a Business Development Director, experienced it.

Internal reaction to a negative belief

Understanding how my negatives beliefs manifested themselves in a negative reaction, that in turn adversely affected my interaction with other people, has proven very useful for me. Recently in starting up my own business I had my first session with the clients I would be working with.

After a restless night in which I woke with a feeling of dread and a series of disastrous scenarios playing out in my head, I remembered amongst other helpful techniques to imagine the session going well.

This gave me the breathing space to relax enough to prepare for the session with the clients.

I did come up against some resistance that morning, but because I had let a more positive outcome into my thinking earlier in the day, I had in my subconscious the belief that there was a way to push on.

I believe this simple technique helped me to work through the process and succeed. As a footnote the organisation has commissioned a lot more work from me and the project is seen as a great success.

Now that we have dealt with your negative beliefs about your ability to impact on others in a progressively effective manner, let us start working up the continuum of interpersonal skills, step by step.

At each stage I suggest a systematic approach, which will help you to work on your beliefs that an outcome is possible and then provide you with the skills to turn that belief into a reality. If I were coaching a motivated client, I would expect them to take about a year to get from assertiveness to conciliation. So do read the book all the way through, then go back and think about the concepts that I have set out. As you read them, consider your own situations, plan different reactions and start noticing the improved results that you are achieving.

The first step on the continuum of interpersonal skills is to understand the impact of impoverished interpersonal skills.

Working through beliefs and skills

*I have been a deputy director of finance for several years with the same organisation, during which time I have acted up as the director of finance on many occasions. I have always thought that the director role required a range of skills which I didn't possess and therefore had consistently seen myself as a **deputy**. I have confirmed this perception to myself time and time again when things may not have gone well finding comfort in "only being the deputy". This has also led me to avoid challenging and confronting senior colleagues who probably know best!*

I had often considered applying for a director's role and got close on a few occasions after being invited to do so. However, after my last interview performance, which in my view didn't go well, the prospect of another process was not comfortable. Therefore, I managed to scupper my initial momentum in applying for posts by developing a range of excuses. I think we have all found them whilst trying to avoid something. They include "I'm too busy with work", "It's not the right time", etc. It is relatively easy to find excuses for not doing anything and it is often less easy to find reasons for doing things that are outside of your comfort zone.

*I recently met Pam after she was recommended by a senior director of finance who had been coached by her for many years and linked his development and success to the techniques and advice she gave him. He had seen potential in me and questioned why I was not applying for director-level posts. I found several creative responses which I was pleased with and thirty minutes later we both concluded that the real reasons was **apathy**, a lack of confidence and even the thought of the prospect of greater responsibility was daunting.*

I was apprehensive before meeting Pam as I didn't know what to expect. As an accountant, I was ready to justify my perceptions about the additional skills required in being a director and conclusively outline my weaknesses and shortfalls so my case was clear. In some way, I think I would have been satisfied if Pam had agreed with me and developed my arguments. This would have helped me bounce future opportunities more professionally. However, what Pam did was much more uncomfortable: she asked me to recognise and quantify my strengths and attributes. It is hard doing this at the best of times, but accountants are trained to be prudent and look on the downside and I have become good at this when viewing my own performance. It therefore took some time for me to realise the strengths that I had and how to best to present them to other people.

She then went on to tackle the negative beliefs that I had built up over many years which were interrupting my performance and potential advancement. Everyone has these. However the successful person develops a positive belief system. This affects performance positively reversing the negative process we all have. I have found the beliefs and skills approach in her book invaluable.

Pam's strategies and concepts helped my performance at work and this was noticed. I was less quick to compromise – to avoid potential conflict where the compromise was clearly not the best solution. I now saw myself in a different light, applied for a director's post and was appointed. Because I can focus and expand on my new found strengths I am now confident of following through.

It's still early days and I have a lot to learn as I work my way up "the continuum of interpersonal skills". I strongly recommend this approach which I believe will benefit anyone seeking to improve their general performance in all aspects of their life.

Having read the section on changing negative beliefs, it is possible that this chapter prompted you to look at some difficult issues. The following questions will assist you to process your reactions to what you have just read.

Reactionnaire

1. What were your thoughts as you read the sections on negative beliefs?

2. What were your feelings as you read the **What's the point of trying, when I am just to be tolerated initially and then rejected?'** example?

3. What ideas popped into your head as you read the negative beliefs example?

4. What actions did you feel inclined to take as a result of reading the negative beliefs section?

5. What negative beliefs do you hold about yourself and your ability to interact with other people?

a)

b)

c)

Taking one of these examples. Complete the diagram below to reveal what impact that holding this negative belief may have on your behaviour?

The cycle of negative beliefs

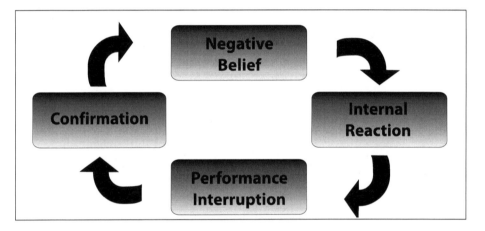

What negative belief have you highlighted that has the effect of interrupting your performance?

Internal reactions – what do you think as you approach situations or people that stimulate your negative belief about yourself?

Performance interruption - how do you interrupt your performance when you are in a difficult situation or in the presence of people that you find difficult?

Confirmation – when you walk away from situations or interactions you find difficult and you have performed badly - what do you tend to say to yourself which confirms the original negative belief that you held?

What reactions do you have to what you have just written?

When doing this exercise, it is important to remember that you are not creating these thoughts and reactions, you are simply shining a light on them. It can be quite shocking to realise that you have these thoughts always circling around in the background of your mind. When you are aware of them and the impact they have on your performance you are in a much better position to reverse the negative effect of them.

1. What were your thoughts as you read the sections on positive beliefs?

2. What were your feelings as you read the **'People will accept me because I am good enough'**. Example?

3. What ideas popped into your head as you read the positive beliefs example?

4. What actions did you feel inclined to take as a result of reading the positive beliefs section?

5. What positive beliefs would you like to hold about yourself and your ability to interact with other people?
a)

b)

c)

Taking one of these examples. Complete the diagram below to reveal what impact holding this more positive belief may have on your performance?

The cycle of positive beliefs

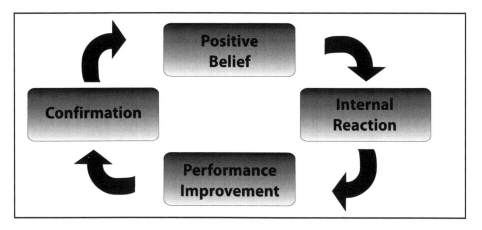

What positive belief have you highlighted that would have the effect of improving your performance?

Internal reactions – what would you think about approaching situations or people if you held this positive belief about yourself?

Performance improvement – if you held this more positive belief about yourself – how would you improve your performance when you are in a difficult situation or in the presence of people that you find difficult?

Confirmation – when you walk away from a situation or interaction and you have improved your performance – what would you say to yourself which confirms the positive belief that you are starting to hold?

What reactions do you have to what you have just written?

> Now turn to page 187, Annex 1, to
> explore your negative and positive beliefs
> in sample chapters from the *People Skills*
> *Revolution Companion Workbook.* ..

Chapter 4

Impoverished
Interpersonal Skills

The Continuum of Interpersonal Skills – Impoverished Skills

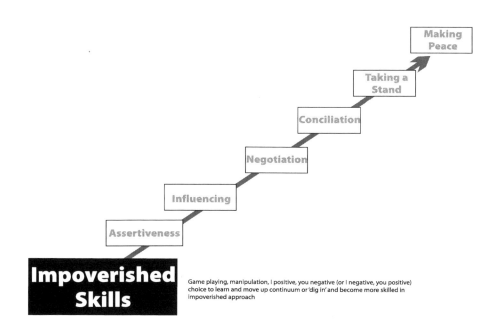

Making
Peace

Taking a
Stand

Conciliation

Negotiation

Influencing

Assertiveness

**Impoverished
Skills**

Game playing, manipulation, I positive, you negative (or I negative, you positive)
choice to learn and move up continuum or 'dig in' and become more skilled in
impoverished approach

Rather than dwell on poor interpersonal skills and their consequences, I would like to define them. For me, impoverished interpersonal skills include:

- game playing
- manipulation
- bullying
- seeing yourself as better or worse in relation to someone else.

Let's face it, we have all done at least one of these things to some extent to get our needs met.

Usually, impoverished skills are learnt behaviour, acquired during the socialisation process. Although people may not feel very confident or in control, most people do not realise that the cause of their problem is their poor interpersonal skills combined with a negative outlook on life. Instead they are doing the best they can with the resources that they have at their disposal. So, in other words, I think it is important not to blame others for behaving in a way that demonstrates impoverished skills.

Developing the skills I outline in this book will help you to become more honest and effective in your dealings with others and, in the process, will help you to achieve your needs using a more direct approach. As your confidence and sense of control increase, people's ability to manipulate or play games with you will decrease significantly.

Having said that, people do continually do things that have a negative impact on others. So before we go on to skills building, I want to share two concepts with you that I found very useful.

- Whatever someone does, it is not about you.
- Look after yourself and the relationship will take care of itself – one way or another.

It's not about you

When I first heard the phrase 'Whatever someone does, it is not about you', I was highly doubtful. If I promote the idea of cause and effect in terms of human behaviour, it follows that when I take an action, it is either as a stimulus or as a response to a situation. While I do agree with this premise – and promote it in this book – I want to explore an alternative interpretation: that you do not always cause the behaviour of others.

Let me show you what I mean by using an example. I see myself as a friendly and approachable person. If you met me, I would be friendly and approachable with you too. So if I come across you and am friendly and approachable with you, is this because you have created this in me or is it because it's my usual style? Obviously, it is my usual style.

Now imagine someone is rude and aggressive to you. It is possible that you have done something to upset them, but it is more likely that they are rude and aggressive to a lot of people. You just happen to have crossed their path.

I once had a boss who bullied me so severely that I took time off with stress, along with about four other people. At the time, of course, I took that very personally, but when you think about it, this said more about the boss than me – I just happened to be in the wrong place at the wrong time. Since that time I have never experienced any problems in my interactions with bosses or colleagues. Learn not to dwell on, or react to, random irrational comments or incidents from one person, which may trigger a negative belief about yourself.

If you want to learn about your behaviour from the feedback of others, look for – and take note of – patterns of comments from a range of people.

Look after yourself

The second concept I would like you to consider is 'Look after yourself and the relationship will take care of itself – one way or another'. On my programmes I often hear comments like: 'It's not me who should be here, it's my manager'. When faced with an interpersonal challenge, the key message is: 'The only person's behaviour you can change is your own'. Change your behaviour, and the other person will be compelled to respond differently to you.

When we find ourselves in a difficult relationship, it is so tempting to want to understand the motives of the other person. This is a waste of energy. As someone once said: 'It's a bit like trying to teach a pig to sing. It doesn't work and it irritates the pig.'

Using these skills will stop people manipulating, bullying and playing games with you in nearly every instance you can imagine, until you get towards the very top of the continuum of interpersonal skills (see page 39). Here I have noticed that some of my highly skilled clients come across characters that they just do not know how to handle. These people cause great disruption to my clients and the organisations they work with.

Sometimes, after hours of discussion, we have been able jointly to piece together a way forward, which has been extremely effective. This has happened so often that I also consider this to be a pattern. So towards the end of this book I describe how to deal with these high-level manipulators (see Chapter 11).

If you are around one of these people, you will feel uncomfortable and your emotions will be heightened. You may notice that things are 'blowing up' around you or that you are using a lot more energy to achieve very little – you might even feel as if you are going backwards. You will notice yourself losing control and a charming but elusive person gaining it without any logical basis for this increasing powerbase. These arch manipulators often appear suddenly, do not go through the usual recruitment process, claim overseas experience, sound highly plausible, make themselves indispensable to the leader of the organisation and create chaos in the name of streamlining structures or services.

In Chapter 11 I will talk about these characters. I will tell you how to spot them, how to identify their behaviour and what to do not to get caught up in the whirlwind and chaos that they create.

These are not people who get their needs met through others on an occasional basis; these are people who study the art of manipulation in the same way that I will be helping you to study the positive art of people skills.

The underlying reason for impoverished interpersonal skills is a lack of balance in the way we see ourselves. To achieve effective interpersonal skills, you must regard yourself and others as equals. The most effective way to do this is to become more assertive.

Now turn to page 197, Annex 1, to explore your experience of impoverished interpersonal skills in the sample chapters from the *People Skills Revolution* Workbook.

Chapter 5

Assertiveness

The Continuum of Interpersonal Skills – Assertiveness

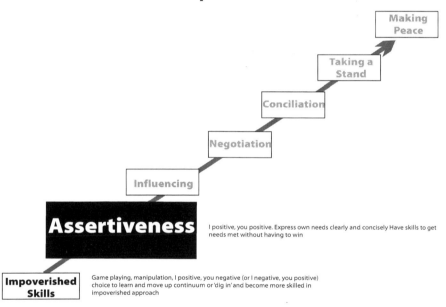

Most people are not happy to hear that they need to learn some basic assertiveness skills, but from my experience when people run into problems while interacting with others, a lack of assertiveness is at the root of the issue. This is true of even the most senior staff and also those people with the most apparently sophisticated interpersonal skills.

I have seen whole organisational transformation programmes unravel when the new chief executive officer wants to be liked and cannot say 'no', and when board-level managers are manipulated into time-consuming and energy-sapping dramas by people who pursue their own personal agendas at all costs.

Assertiveness skills bulletproof people against manipulation.

So, whether you are a government minister who can't say 'no' when pressured by a colleague to increase the budget for your department, or a production manager who is always helpfully changing shifts to suit the company while your counterpart has time to network with people and has an active social life, you might find some basic assertiveness skills incredibly useful.

Devised in the 1970s, assertiveness skills training has improved the lives of millions of people. It was also the first step that I took on the path of self-development. When working as a training professional for an international drug company, I was asked to run an assertiveness skills workshop. I thought that before I ran the course, I needed to find out more about it. Thinking that I had no assertiveness issues, I joined a programme that met each week for two hours. During this ten-week period, I had a number of significant 'light bulb' moments and realised that I was not quite as assertive as I had imagined. Now, having worked in the personal development field for over 20 years, I believe that no one is quite as assertive as they think they are – or would like to be.

I cannot tell you the number of people with many years of working experience who have come up to me after an assertiveness programme and said 'I wish I had known all of this when I was younger' or 'They should really be teaching these skills in school'. I agree with both these statements. Learning how to interact with others in a non-judgemental and productive manner should be part of the curriculum, and everyone at work should be obliged to develop these skills. This would prevent a great deal of the game-playing and bullying that takes place in organisations. It would also create a language and diagnostic tool for identifying ineffective interpersonal behaviour.

The basic premise behind assertiveness is that you should respect yourself and others. Where things go wrong with this very simple idea is that we may be passive, constantly deferring to other people or allowing them to manipulate us, or we may be aggressive and put our needs above those of others most of the time. Neither of these positions is healthy or conducive to a successful working and living environment.

It is important to say that no one is wholly passive and no one is wholly aggressive, but we do have tendencies towards one end of the spectrum.

People who have a tendency towards passivity think that life is 'being done to them'; they feel like an 'extra' rather than the central character in their own play. They tend to come across as a victim and they might experience illnesses like ulcers and depression.

In contrast, people with a tendency towards aggression take the centre stage. They are the most important person and just see others as the bit part actors in their dramas. They tend to come across as dominant and selfish. In terms of their health, they are inclined to have heart attacks and high blood pressure.

Although people generally understand the difference between passivity and aggression, one of the most difficult aspects of assertiveness is to understand what it is. When I used to talk to managers about the training needs of staff and I suggested an assertiveness course, they would often look horrified and say 'but they are too assertive already'. This gave me a very good indication that they did not understand the basic premise behind the approach. When I said assertiveness, they heard aggressiveness. Also, passive people look at aggressive people and think, 'If that is assertiveness, I would rather not bother'. Equally, aggressive people look at people who have a tendency to be passive and say, 'I would not like to be like that'.

So it is important to clarify from the outset what the difference is between passive, aggressive and assertive behaviour.

- Passivity is when people habitually defer to the needs of others.
- Aggression is when people constantly put their own needs above the needs of others.
- Assertiveness is when people take positive action to get their needs met and allow others to do the same.

People who have a tendency to be passive:
- use deferential language like 'It's only my opinion, but …'
- feel uncomfortable making eye contact
- tend not to be clear about what they want
- get easily sidetracked
- are susceptible to flattery
- criticise others behind their back
- talk in a timid and apologetic voice
- don't take up their full body space and slouch to appear smaller.

In assertiveness training language, one very common way of expressing this is 'I negative, you positive'.

In contrast, people who have a tendency to be aggressive:

- use language like 'I don't care what you think. Do it or else'
- maintain eye contact which just feels too long
- raise their voice to get attention or talk over people
- move into other people's personal space
- tend not to listen to what is being said
- criticise the behaviour and intentions of others
- feel uncomfortable when they do not get their own way.

This stance can be expressed as 'I positive, you negative'.

'I positive, you positive'

Assertiveness is different, because it involves adopting an 'I positive, you positive' position.

Assertive people tend to:

- use involving language like 'This is my opinion, what do you think?'
- make comfortable eye contact
- adopt a relaxed and open body posture and natural tone of voice
- take up their full space and respect the personal space of others
- use their interpersonal skills to express their needs and ideas
- allow other people to express their needs and ideas.

The assertive person believes that people are equal to him or her and that they can have a huge influence on their interactions with other people. They can accept that events do not always work out the way they would like, because due to their interpersonal skills, they can ensure that most of the time they do. They have the capability to achieve the outcomes they want, while enabling others to be comfortable and relaxed around them. They also encourage and allow others to achieve their goals.

On one of my courses I ask people whom they admire and who is effective in their eyes. The people they select display the same characteristics. They are considered to be principled, fair, consistent personalities, with clear boundaries, who respect other people, take the time to listen and encourage the development of others. Although no doubt these people have many of the sophisticated and effective people skills I will cover later on in the book, they have a fundamental 'I positive, you positive' viewpoint backed up with the basic underpinning assertiveness skills.

It is human nature to avoid additional work or effort, particularly when it is not central to our primary role. To reduce our workload, we will tend to go to the person who is prepared to meet our needs or requests in the easiest way possible.

We all have a tendency to do this. So do not blame the person who is constantly asking you to do something rather than someone else in the office. Instead look at the reasons why that might be. If you always have a tendency to say 'yes' to a request and the person sitting next to you has a tendency to say 'yes' sometimes and 'no' sometimes, you should not be surprised if the person making the request keeps on coming to you. It is only natural to go to the person who is going to put up the least resistance, so that the person making the request can then move on to other tasks. You should not then be surprised when your level of work becomes very high and others get to operate within their budgets, have a planned social life, are free to undertake networking activities and go home on time.

Personal boundaries are the point at which you end and others begin. If you are not able to identify and hold your own boundaries, you will never be able to say 'no' to the requests of others. If you cannot say 'no', then your time, money and resources have the potential to become their time, money and resources.

When this happens, at some level we know we have been 'had' and we resent it. We may feel this in the pit of our stomach when we have accepted work or responsibilities that we know should not have been ours. In reality though, we have created this situation by not having clear boundaries and by not using effective interpersonal skills to protect those boundaries.

To identify whether you need to be more assertive, let's look at the 'I positive, you positive' concept more closely. The idea of 'I positive, you positive' is so central to achieving more effective outcomes that I want to reflect on what it means. Put simply, it means that if you spend most of your day thinking that other people are village idiots (I positive, you negative) who have to be controlled or ridiculed, you probably have an assertiveness issue to address. Equally, if you spend all day resenting other people or feeling that they are out to get you, you are probably taking the victim (I negative, you positive) stance. In this case, you will be permanently on your guard, waiting for the next bad thing to happen. Both of these views can be very stressful positions to take. The 'I positive, you positive' position involves identifying and respecting your own needs and goals and taking action to enable those needs and goals to be achieved in a direct and honest manner and allowing other people to do the same.

So how do you know when things are wrong in your interactions with others? I think you know when you feel a general unease around some people. This might mean that you feel under intense pressure to support a course of action that you feel uncomfortable about, you perceive yourself to be doing all the work, or other people are constantly getting money or other resources out of you or deciding how you should spend your time. Another sign that things are seriously out of balance is when you are always going out of your way to help people and these favours are not reciprocated.

The concept of trading stamps can be very helpful here. Trading stamps became popular during the Great Depression of the 1930s. They were printed stamps which were given out when goods were purchased. They could be saved and pasted into booklets until the individual collecting them had a sufficient number to exchange them for a particular item of merchandise. In the context of behaviour, when someone does something that we feel uneasy about, we often rationalise the situation by saying, 'It is only a small incident and it is not worth bothering about'. We think we have 'let this go'. But we do not let it go. Instead, each time we are feeling uncomfortable about something that has happened, we collect a 'stamp' and put it in our 'book'. When we have a full book, we 'cash them in'. This is why an apparently unassuming person can act completely out of character – perhaps screaming at the top of their voice in the middle of the office about something really insignificant. It is not only that incident that they are screaming about. Rather, it is the cumulative effect of all the other incidents that have happened which they have decided not to act upon (but instead subconsciously collected a 'stamp' about). Often, the intensity of the reaction in relation to the event is not only shocking to colleagues, friends and family, but it can also be shocking to the person who has this reaction, especially if they have a tendency to regard themselves as very passive. Embarrassed by their outburst, they can become even more determined to control their emotions rather than acting on them, making a lack of assertiveness a self-reinforcing circle.

At the other end of the assertiveness spectrum there are the people who have a tendency to be aggressive (I positive, you negative). Operating mostly from this position people may get their needs met, but they notice that no one is around to celebrate their success with them. These people appear in coaching situations and on assertiveness courses much less often. This could be because it takes a brave person to tell an aggressive person that there might be something lacking in their behaviour. Interestingly, when they do appear willingly on courses, I have found that they are remarkably motivated to change. I think this is because they are isolated. We are all human animals who need the company and attention of others. The aggressive person experiences a world in which they get what they want most of the time, but when they walk in the door most of their colleagues or family walk out of the other exit. Getting what you want can be a hollow victory, when you are sitting there on your own.

Luckily, in my working and personal life I have met few people who I consider to be manipulative. By 'manipulative' I mean people who deliberately set out to achieve their goals through devious means. In terms of the 'I positive, you positive' model they are clearly at the aggressive (I positive, you negative) end of the scale. Manipulative people can be very difficult to deal with in a work situation. They are often at the centre of dramas. If I am coaching them, they can be utterly charming, flattering even, can say all the right things and commit to take different actions. When you next meet them they have rarely done any of them, although they will remain positive and upbeat about the work we are doing together. They will continue to come to the sessions until I get bored or I challenge them on an aspect of their behaviour. At this point, people who have a tendency to be manipulative have a choice: they can either do what most people do when faced with difficult feedback – test the validity of the comments with other people and decide whether or not to act on them – or they 'shoot the messenger' and commit to getting better at concealing their agendas.

Inherited behaviours

Whether we have a tendency to be aggressive, passive or manipulative, it is usually learnt behaviour that we pick up in childhood. Some families promote the concept 'Don't let anyone grind you down, while others say, 'You cannot trust anyone outside your family'. These two stances, or the thousands of other messages that we pick up when we are forming our character, will have a huge impact on our interactions with other people. Just before you go blaming your mother for your unpopularity at work, remember that messages and behaviours are passed down the family line and that your parents picked up these stances in the same way that you did.

I have a story to tell you about inherited behaviour. A young woman was cooking a ham. As she was putting it into the oven, her partner said to her, 'Why have you cut off the end of the ham?'. Looking bemused, she said, 'My mother always did it that way and the flavour was lovely'. Next time she was at her mother's, she asked her why she cut off the end of the ham and her mother said, 'Well, my mother did it that way'. Speaking to her grandmother a few weeks later, the young woman remembered to ask her why she cut the end off the ham. Her grandmother laughed and said, 'Well that's obvious, dear, if you don't cut the end off the ham, it won't fit in the pan'.

Much of our behaviour is like cutting the end off the ham before we put it in the pan. We do it habitually and without thinking – we have just assimilated it into our own bundle of habits. Assertiveness is a process that lets us stand back from our unconscious patterns and make some different decisions about how we approach our interactions with other people.

Assertiveness skills are a set of simple tools and techniques, which enable people to avoid 'collecting stamps' by tackling events as they arise. This is achieved by introducing a logical thought process to interrupt their automatic patterns of stimulus and response. In changing their behaviour to achieve different outcomes, people enhance their self-esteem and improve their interpersonal relationships by respecting themselves and respecting others.

How we see others is a reflection of our core beliefs about ourselves and the world. The assertiveness toolkit will help you to achieve more positive outcomes and should reinforce the, 'I positive, you positive' position.

My early attempts to try out the new techniques I had learnt – with my boss, colleagues, relatives and friends – were incredibly clumsy, but they did lay the foundations for the incremental skills-building process that I have set out in this book. I mention this because when my clients first start to use the techniques, they report feeling very uncomfortable and the results can appear fragmented. They experience success in some situations but on other occasions just become more aware of what they could have done differently after the event. This is perfectly normal. As your awareness increases you will start to notice more incidents when you would like to become more assertive. As your skills develop, the time between your awareness and taking action will shorten until you will begin to anticipate what you need to do to get your needs and goals met in an honest and direct manner as each interaction unfolds.

It is important to realise that you are learning a new skill. It may seem very mechanical and awkward to start with. Keep going, it will get easier the more you identify your intentions and pursue them in a clear, concise and unemotional way without getting sidetracked by predictable deflections.

The success gained from this section on enhancing your assertiveness will be built on in the later chapters of the book. However, if you never manage to fully adopt, or work towards, this 'I positive, you positive' stance and you continue to build your interpersonal skills along the lines I outline, you will, I believe, be learning to manipulate rather than to influence – just with more tools at your disposal. The positive aspect of this perspective is that the same tools do not seem to be as effective in the hands of the manipulators, nor do they appear to achieve the incremental skills build and associated benefits that I suggest are possible when working through the continuum of interpersonal skills.

Just take a few moments to consider how many times a day you take an 'I positive, you negative' or 'You positive, I negative' position. What do these reflections say about how you perceive yourself and other people?

The assertiveness toolkit

There are four stages to having an assertive interaction:

- **Stage 1** – decide to achieve a different outcome and be clear about what success would look like
- **Stage 2** – explain your position clearly and concisely in a logical manner without showing emotion or using emotional language
- **Stage 3** – use the assertiveness techniques to avoid getting sidetracked from achieving your aim
- **Stage 4** – acknowledge and accept that when you first start to achieve different outcomes, you may feel guilty or uncomfortable for a short while afterwards.

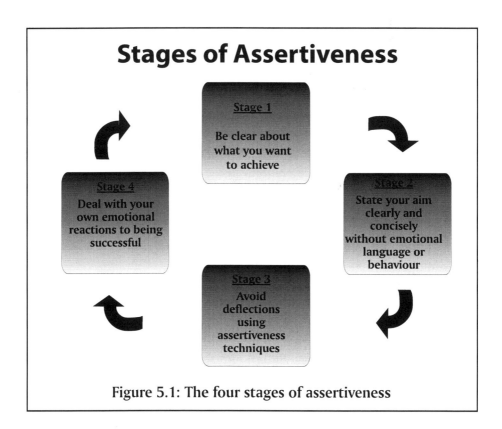

Figure 5.1: The four stages of assertiveness

Stage 1: Be clear about your needs and what you want to achieve

When people lack confidence or assertiveness skills, they often stop having needs.

As children we all have needs. When we state these needs and get our needs met, we continue to have needs and expect them to be met. Imagine, however, a child who has needs but rarely gets those needs met. In the end it would be better to have no needs than to suffer the discomfort of constant disappointment. In this instance we would turn off our antenna that is constantly informing us of our needs. It just makes life easier. At this point the child may even believe that they have no needs. So one of the first tasks in assisting someone to be more assertive is to get them reacquainted with their needs.

When I went on my own assertiveness course, I did not believe that I had many issues to deal with. As the course progressed, I realised that one of the reasons that I did not have requests turned down is that I rarely made them. Somewhere along the line I had lost touch with my needs. I envied the people who had loads of preferences about everything. I tended to accept what I had and what life gave to me. This was a very hard discovery. Somehow I had to find me again and to work out what I wanted from life and what my preferences were. My first steps were really small. I began to notice that my friend was borrowing things from me but not returning them, so gradually I was being dispossessed of items that I considered precious. This stopped me from enthusing about anything in front of her, in case she decided to ask me if she could borrow it. On the assertiveness course, I realised that I could firstly say 'no' to her requests and secondly start asking her to return the things that she had borrowed.

Now this may not sound that difficult to you. When developing assertiveness, you need to realise that what makes **you** less effective may not be what makes **me** less effective. We all have different things that create blocks for us. Yours might be saying 'no' to a boss who pressures you into doing something that is against your principles, or saying 'no' to a manager who asks you to increase the funding for his or her department. We all have different blocks, and what might be easy for one person might be very difficult for another person. So do not assume that just because you can ask for a raise or promotion that other people can as well. Equally, you might be able to say 'no' to your boss, but might find it extremely difficult to say 'no' to your mother.

Assertiveness is firstly about knowing what you want to achieve and then taking the action to make it much more likely that the desired situation will happen. One of the best ways to start getting reacquainted with your needs is to start to notice those moments of unease when you just know that you are not happy about something that has occurred. The more you start to notice those situations, the more you will start to identify your needs.

This may involve saying 'no' to people when you used to say 'yes', asking people to do something for you instead, or dealing with people who are able to tie up your time, money and emotions.

Stage 2: State your needs clearly and concisely without using emotional language or behaviour

Once you have made the decision to achieve different outcomes, the next stage is to state your intention clearly and concisely without using emotional content.

Assertiveness is a very logical, rational approach, which uses emotions to inform how you interact with others, rather than talking in emotional language or displaying emotional behaviour.

Keep this step simple. When you go into too much detail, you give the other person the opportunity to 'hook' onto the information you have given and use it to deflect you from your path.

Wouldn't it be lovely, if you made a decision to approach a situation differently and you explained your new course of action and everyone said, 'That's great, you have been a doormat for too long. I am glad you are finally standing up for yourself'? Unfortunately, life is not usually like that.

If you have had a tendency to be passive and to do what others want, they will resist your attempts to climb 'out of the box' they have put you in. They like what you do to assist them and they are not going to let you off the hook that easily. So learn to deal with the very predictable deflections that come with the decision to behave differently.

Stage 3: Deal with deflections

If you have always done what people ask of you, they will have had no need to try to persuade you or make you feel guilty. So when you try to change your behaviour, it can come as a surprise to find out that people will try to make it difficult for you to change your behaviour and will try to deflect you from your path.

Deflections take two main forms – flattery and criticism. As a general rule, people will try flattery first and if that does not work, they will move on to criticism. At the first hint of resistance, people usually try flattery to get us to change our minds. If you have a tendency to be passive, the following statements might even sound very familiar to you:

> *'Oh, but you have always been so helpful before.'*
> *'I tell everyone what a lovely and helpful person you are.'*
> *'You are not going to let me down are you? I rely so much on you for support.'*

For a lot of people who like to be liked, these statements can be enough to keep them doing what they have always done in the past and make them forget the idea of being assertive, because the person asking is being so nice to them. If they maintain their resolve, however, and decide to say 'no', something rather unexpected starts to happen: they start to get criticised.

People who usually say 'yes' are not normally criticised, so it can come as an unpleasant shock when they are criticised for standing their ground. The sort of critical comments you might expect might include:

> *'What do you mean you can't do it?'*
> *'But I thought we were friends (or allies).'*
> *'But you have always been so helpful in the past.'*
> *'This is just not like you – I have always relied on you for support and now you are letting me down.'*
> *'I am sure you can change your arrangements for* **me**.*'*

For the passive person who likes to be liked, none of these phrases is easy to hear. But realising the predictability of these deflections can help you to deal with them. One golden rule is that the moment you start to engage in conversation and respond to the deflections in any way, that is the moment when you lose control of the conversation. Nor should you make alternative suggestions to help them to solve their problem. They will 'hook' onto these ideas to get you back into the dialogue, and before you know it they will be asking you to meet their request again.

So, when people say, 'Oh but you've always been so helpful in the past', thank them for their remark but do not allow it to move you off your path. Equally, when they say, 'But you used to be so helpful', acknowledge that this is true and go back to stating your aim clearly and concisely, without using emotional language or behaviour.

When people say, 'But I was relying on you', don't mention anyone else who may be able to help or make alternative suggestions as to how their problem can be solved. Instead, say 'I would help if I could, but on this occasion I can't'.

You can use a number of standard assertiveness techniques to deal with the inevitable deflections that will come when you try to change your behaviour. These assertiveness techniques are:

- broken record
- fogging
- negative assertion
- negative enquiry.

Broken record

The 'broken record' assertiveness technique involves restating your aims when you are making a request or being challenged. It is a very useful technique for avoiding getting drawn into any arguments or debates. Children are experts at using the broken record technique. If they want some sweets in a supermarket, they will keep stating the same words until they get what they want. As adults, this would be very unattractive behaviour. Used with a bit more subtlety, however, it can be an effective way to maintain resolve and to buy valuable thinking time.

For example, suppose you are a board-level manager who is constantly being asked to provide additional resources for a project. In the past you might have got drawn into the argument and been flattered by the comments of the other party regarding your efficiency and dedication to providing an excellent service to customers. You might also have felt a pang of unease when they mentioned how others might react when they hear how unhelpful you have been.

Broken record allows you to restate your purpose without getting sidetracked by these predictable deflections. Of course, you can soften your response by making statements like 'I do understand you have a job to do' and then follow it with '… but on this occasion I am not able to help you'.

After a while, most people get the hint that you are not going to be drawn into the discussion with them. If they persist and you keep using the broken record technique, you might begin to look a bit robotic and they might wonder if there is something wrong with you. So if the broken record technique does not work after a series of attempts to maintain your resolve, try combining your responses with one of the other assertiveness techniques for dealing with criticism: fogging, negative assertion and negative enquiry.

Fogging

The 'fogging' assertiveness technique involves allowing what the other person says to just 'hang in the air' and not feel the need to defend or attack. One way to do this is to find some limited truth in what the person has said, perhaps by saying something like: 'I can see that it might look like that from your perspective'. Now this does not sound as if it would work, but in fact it can be very effective. Although it appears that you are agreeing with them, you are in fact agreeing that they are entitled to their own assessment of the situation, which of course we all are.

So when someone tells you that the project must go ahead and that you are being obstructive and just don't understand all the facts or have obviously not read the supporting papers, just say something like: 'I can see that it might seem that way to you'. Often people will think you are agreeing with them and sigh with relief, but in fact you are actually agreeing that they are entitled to their perspective on the situation.

Fogging avoids defending or attacking and can be remarkably effective in avoiding situations escalating out of control. If, however, you keep fogging despite the other party's increasing attempts to goad you into an argument, they might find your lack of reaction rather strange. In which case, you might find the techniques of negative assertion or negative enquiry useful.

Negative assertion

With the 'negative assertion' technique you agree with the aspects of any criticism of your behaviour that are true, acknowledging that we cannot all be good at everything. We tend to do 'negative assertion' naturally with people we are comfortable with. This approach 'takes the wind out of the sails' of the critic and avoids the interaction ending in an argument with you counter-attacking or putting yourself down.

So, if the other person shouts at you and says that 'you have clearly not read all of the documentation for the project approval process', you could say: 'Yes, on this occasion I have not had time to read the papers [negative assertion], but I am still not able to support your request for funding for this project [broken record]'.

Negative enquiry

Sometimes it is obvious that despite all your attempts to defuse the situation, the criticism is not going to go away and might even get worse. If you have already used the other techniques without success, this will have bought you some thinking time. Now find out more information and ask the critic what it is, specifically, that they are bothered about. It might be that they have difficulty giving feedback to others (many people do). By asking them to be more specific about their complaint, you can open up lines of communication and gain more information on the areas of your behaviour that fall below their expectations, or find out more about what it is that is of concern to them.

This is what one client, a director of finance, wrote about her ability to see deflections when previously she tended to get drawn in by them.

> *'Using the techniques I can now spot this so easily in discussions – particularly in difficult conversations. I have learnt to – no matter how much a deflection it is – crucially not to respond or be dragged in. Instead I politely acknowledge a point but bring the conversation back to my agenda. Being familiar with deflection tactics means you can spot the signals and will have prepared techniques to manage them. This avoids losing control of the conversation, avoids emotional conversation. Means you stay on the periphery of a disastrous situation rather than in the middle of it.'*

Stage 4: Deal with the reactions to success

The last stage to being more assertive may surprise you. I have found over the years that what stops people being more assertive is the often uncomfortable feelings of guilt they experience when they do change their behaviour and gain a successful outcome. They achieve what they want, but somehow do not feel good about themselves in the process. Of course, the other person may well assist you to feel guilty with their deflective flattery, but mostly it is an internal response to putting yourself and your needs first.

Remember that feeling guilty is part of the process – sit with it, know that you have achieved something positive and appreciate that for the time it took you to say 'no' you have probably gained hours of time for yourself or taken control of your corporate or personal wallet.

The assertiveness techniques in action

So let's show the use of this model in a typical 'saying no' situation.

A departmental head keeps on asking you (their manager) for additional funding. Although you want to say 'no', they always put up such a good argument for why you should support them, that you have always said 'yes'. You now realise that this has led to some random decisions being made and that expenditure has been skewed in favour of that department.

The board has agreed that no further expenditure should be made without a comprehensive business case, but you know that this person can be aggressive or manipulative. You also know your own tendency to want to be liked.

1. Make the decision that the next time you are approached to approve additional funding, you will say 'no'. Consider how you will express this to the person who makes the request (Stage 1 – be clear about what you want to achieve).

2. State (to whoever makes the approach) that all new expenditure must have a business case (Stage 2 – state your aim clearly and concisely without using emotional language or behaviour).

3. So far so good. But then the aggressive or manipulative departmental head starts trying to deflect you from your purpose. Deal with these deflections by using the assertiveness techniques (Stage 3 – avoid deflections using assertiveness techniques).

The conversation might go as follows:

Department head (DH): *'You have always been so supportive of this department and the quality of our work has improved so much as a result – it certainly seems to have earned you positive press coverage …' (Flattery)*

You: *'Thank you, I appreciate the compliments, but – as I said before – to justify more funding for your department, you must have a business case.' (Broken record)*

DH: *'Oh dear, have you become such a weak leader these days that you are afraid of your own shadow and feel compelled to kowtow to the organisational "powers that be"?' (Criticism)*

You: *'I know it might seem that way sometimes, but to agree expenditure I need a business plan.' (Fogging and broken record)*

DH: *'Well I must say, you have become a shadow of your former self.' (Criticism)*

You *(by now you are probably a bit put out by these comments, but you are also aware that going on the defensive, or on the attack, will probably lead to an argument and result in your losing control*

> *of the interaction):* '*I can understand that it may seem that way to you these days.' (Fogging)*
>
> **DH:** '*It's just ridiculous, you have just sprung this idea on us without any notice. You do realise that we have a business to run here?'*
>
> **You:** '*Yes, I would have liked to have given you a bit more notice.' (Negative assertion)*
>
> *[Most people would just give up at this point, since you have not risen to the bait, but the DH carries on in the same vein of criticising and insulting you.]*
>
> **You:** '*What exactly is it about me asking you to do a business plan that is causing you problems?' (Negative enquiry)*
>
> **DH:** '*I don't have the expertise for doing business plans'; or 'This funding requirement is too urgent for lots of paperwork.'*

Whatever the response to your negative enquiry, it enables you to see that either the DH's comments are manipulative or they just need further assistance to comply with your request.

4. Finally, if you feel guilty or uncomfortable after achieving your goals, this is entirely to be expected (Stage 4 – deal with the reactions to success). Just remember that in the time it took to assert your needs clearly, calmly and honestly, you will have prevented other people from having unreasonable access to your time, resources or budget.

And remember, if anyone has **ever** said 'no' to this type of request, in similar circumstances, it will be possible for **you** to say 'no' to this type of request. You just have to learn the skills to do this with a sense of style. When we move out of our comfort zone, by definition it often feels uncomfortable, so we might want to revert back to how we were before. This is a healthy sign. The more you stay just slightly out of your comfort zone – in your risk zone – the more comfortable it will start to feel. After a while, being able to be assertive in challenging circumstances will just become part of the way you operate.

Saying 'no' can be 'macho'

At this point I think it is also worth mentioning a possible gender bias I have noticed when talking about a lack of assertiveness. Although people generally do not like to 'say no' for fear of upsetting people or not being liked, men often do not like saying 'no' because they are concerned that it opens them up to accusations of weakness or lack of competitiveness.

The desire to appear strong at all times, means that sometimes men can be easily persuaded to respond to an extreme challenge They then get caught up in how they are going to achieve the goal rather than stepping back and considering whether what they are being asked to do is desirable or ethical.

As a result their boss, fellow politicians, comrades in arms and business partners can manipulate them into taking action, which might be dubious business practice.

In order to avoid being manipulated in this way it is important to recognise that saying 'no' appropriately can also be interpreted as decisiveness and demonstrate an air of authority. It will also ensure that you allow you own values to act as your compass as to what is right or wrong rather than allow an organisation or person to decide them for you.

Success breeds success, and the more positive outcomes you achieve, the more likely you are to change your behaviour again. This in turn will reinforce a positive cycle of beliefs that you can achieve what you want to achieve in your interactions with others.

There is also something interesting about slowing down interactions with people and being more in control. You will start to notice the things that others do which irritate or annoy you. Most of us think that if the irritation is minor, we let it go, because it is not worth bothering about (being passive). But instead what we actually do is store up a grievance (or, to use the trading stamps analogy mentioned earlier in this chapter, we collect a 'stamp' against that person in our 'book' of irritations, and cash the book in when it is full). This is when apparently nice people can be seen screaming in the office about something trivial, such as, 'You stole my Post-it notes!'. It is not just about those particular Post-it notes; it is about all the other Post-it notes that people have walked off with without thinking. This process can in effect turn an apparently passive person into an apparently aggressive person, which will be confusing to both themselves and others. So instead of storing up these frustrations, the confident person who is in control deals with them as they go along.

You can do this by learning to give effective and constructive criticism to people. One of the problems with giving and receiving criticism is that it is often done very badly, leaving both parties wondering what they could have done differently. For most of us, criticism equals confrontation – yet when we think about it, most of our significant learning comes from when someone has had the courage to tell us how our behaviour could be more effective. Let's face it, it is not hard to give poor feedback to people – you just say what you want to say without any regard for the other person or any consideration as to where and when you tell them.

Even with good intentions, most people do not have the skills to give constructive feedback. You can imagine the conversation: 'I'll say that, then they will say that back … I will then say that, then they will say that back … We will end up in an argument, so I think I won't bother.'

The answer is to use a systematic approach to giving feedback that does not damage the relationship and may even make it better. Giving constructive criticism takes skill and judgement. As a course leader once said to me, it is about 'telling the truth with love'.

Giving feedback

What surprises me about the constructive feedback model (below) for giving feedback is how few people know about and use an approach like this. We live at an ever-increasing pace with an ever-increasing population, which will inevitably lead to greater stress. Yet we do not have the skills to tell another person constructively when they are doing something that we find unacceptable. Here are some things to bear in mind when giving someone constructive criticism.

Decide when to give it. Using the trading stamps analogy again, I believe that we all know when we are collecting stamps and when our books are getting full. I get a feeling in the pit of my stomach. Give feedback before this happens. Begin to work out what your own personal triggers are.

Give feedback when you are clear about the issues you want to raise and what you want the other person to stop or start doing. Do it unemotionally and focus only on the behaviour, not the person. Keep the behaviour you want to address recent and be specific about incidents and dates, if possible. Do not use labels or be judgemental. Start the conversation by saying clearly and concisely what the issue is. Avoid long preambles or getting them to guess what the problem might be. Speak for yourself and talk about how the behaviour affects you, not other people. Some people may want you to give feedback on their behalf, but encourage them to give their own feedback directly to the person.

Realise that most people would prefer not to be having this conversation with you, so it would be human nature to try to deflect you from your intention to give constructive criticism. When you explain the issues to them, there are really only two reactions you will get. Either they will say the equivalent of, 'It's not me, it's the others', or they will be shocked and surprised, since they did not realise the impact of their behaviour on you.

You then need to build in an opportunity for them to respond to what you have said. Do this by pausing or asking them what they think about what you have just told them. Once you have found out which of the two reactions you are getting, you can act accordingly. The pause helps you to gauge their reaction and keep control of the conversation. You might have to comfort someone who is upset or pacify someone who is angry. Having a structure helps you keep on track of the process. If you get lost or sidetracked, it enables you to re-focus and pick up the conversation from the point at which it went off at a tangent or where you lost control.

Believe it or not, most people would behave differently if they knew the impact they were having and if they knew how to do something differently. So do not just dump your thoughts on them, but tell them what you would prefer them to do instead.

The constructive feedback model

The approach I suggest is as follows.

1. Explain the situation – 'On … when you did this …'.

2. Explain why you think you need to raise the issue – 'what I felt, or thought about this was first … then…'

3. Outline the impact it had on you, the team, the business or other relevant parties.

4. Pause for a response. This is the most important step in the dialogue, as it enables you to decide whether you can go straight on to your next points or need to reframe some of what you have said until you are sure that they have heard you. You might also want to reassure them that you are happy with other aspects of their work but need to raise this issue with them for the reasons you have outlined.

5. Describe what you would like them to do instead of what they are doing.

6. Explain how this will improve the situation.

7. Ask them to comment on your suggestion or to make alternative ones which might work better.

There are, of course, people who gain pleasure from being difficult and you may not be able to change their behaviour just by giving them constructive feedback. You might still want to tell them about the impact of their behaviour on you, particularly if you manage them. Then at least you know that you have given them the feedback that you need to give them without it escalating into something unpleasant. In a management situation you might also like to write down what you have told them and what you have agreed that they would do differently as a result of your conversation.

This approach will keep you in control and will prevent you from being drawn into difficult and blaming situations. Use it in association with the assertiveness skills discussed above to stop yourself being sidetracked or deflected from your intention.

So a typical conversation about lateness between you and a member of staff might go something like this:

Stage 1: Explain the situation

You: *'Last Tuesday I noticed that you were 10 minutes late for work. I also noticed that on Thursday you were 20 minutes late for work.'*

Stage 2: Explain why you think you need to raise the issue

You: *'I need to mention this, because it had an impact on the rest of the team and detracts from the level of service that we are able to provide.'*

Stage 3: Outline the impact that their behaviour had on you, the team, the business or other relevant parties

You: *'Sarah had to stay on late to cover for you and Mike missed his appointment at the Regional Office. You will remember that Stella and Sarah both rang you to find out where you were, but your phone kept going to voicemail. In addition a number of your clients rang up asking for you and we were not sure when you would be in.'*

Stage 4: Pause for a response or invite a reaction

You: *'I wonder if you have any comments to make on what I have just told you?'*

As I mentioned above, it is likely that this conversation will elicit one of two responses.

- They will either say something like, 'It was only a few minutes and I don't know what you are bothering about. Everyone does it from time to time and when you interviewed me, you did say that you valued flexibility within the team. I was just being flexible.' There are a number of hooks embedded into this response, any one of which might get you talking about their agenda and what other people do. These are 'everyone does it', 'you did say that you valued flexibility' and 'I was just being flexible'. If you follow any of these lines of thought, you will be deflected off the course of your discussion. So instead, restate that it is necessary that they come in on time. You might not get them to agree with you that it is a problem, but you should be able to get them to the point where they have heard what you have said. You can then go on to the next stage of the conversation, which is to tell them what you would like them to do instead.
- The other likely response is that people are surprised that you have raised the issue with them. They might have thought that being a few minutes late was genuinely not a problem or they might not have understood what you meant by flexibility. They will usually mumble something, but they are generally ready to accept that you may have a point.

In both instances you are now ready to tell them what you would like them to do instead.

Stage 5: Describe what you would like them to do differently from what they are currently doing

You: *'I need you to be here on time, but if you are going to be late I want you to ring Sarah and let her know the reason you are late and when you will arrive.'*

Stage 6: Explain how this will improve the situation

You: *'This will enable other people to get on with their work and not have to spend time reorganising their busy schedules.'*

Stage 7: Ask them to comment on your suggestion or make alternative ones

You: *'Have you got any comments to make about this suggestion?'*

Then give them the opportunity to comment on what you have said and perhaps come up with other strategies.

This is the type of conversation that a manager might have with a member of staff. The structure still works if you are dealing with a work colleague, a friend or a family member.

A note about praise. You can also use the model I have just described to praise someone. Strangely enough people often find it harder to receive positive feedback than negative feedback and will deflect your attempts to recognise their achievement by saying 'I was only doing my job' or 'it was nothing I would do the same for anyone'. In this way they often underestimate the unique contribution that they make to an organisation or team. By taking the time to give positive feedback in a structured way you significantly increase the chances of them hearing your comments.

When you see someone doing something you like, it is a good idea to comment on it. This way they will realise that you value them and appreciate their efforts. The are also much more likely to do this behaviour again.

When giving feedback it is a matter of finding your own style. Think about the person you are talking to and anticipate how they will react. There is no reason why you cannot say positive things about their performance as you talk to them, particularly if they say something like 'are you saying I am doing a bad job then?' Here it makes sense to reassure them that it is one particular behaviour you are commenting on rather than their overall performance.

If you give praise regularly, genuinely and honestly, when it comes to giving feedback, people will be more ready to hear what you have to say about an aspect of their performance which might be counter productive for them and you.

Turning points

I recently worked with a client who had made very rapid progress but our last session together was a bit of a disaster as she was telling me that she was thinking of taking a grievance against five people. For a coach, particularly during the last session this is your worst nightmare.

During the session I got her to go through each of the five scenarios that had upset her. After a while it was clear that some people were reacting differently to her precisely because she was making progress, for example they were becoming relaxed enough around her to start making some amusing or bantering remarks. Since she was not used to them she felt that they were mocking her in some way. One of her issues was about a member of staff who crossed a professional boundary and another one involved a clerical staff member who she felt had done something inappropriate. She also believed that people were talking about her behind her back.

What I explained to her was that if she went down the grievance route her manager would have to facilitate individual sessions with each member of staff to ask them what had happened. I also explained that the outcome of that would be that she would have to talk to them all individually to see if there was a way forward. I indicated what might be the outcome of the five individual discussions and pointed out to her that she should start to see all of these events in isolation rather than lump them all together.

I then suggested to her that she now had all the skills to deal with these incidents individually and did not need to involve the manager as a third party. I knew that she was very much at a cross roads between choosing to become more assertive or continuing to feel disempowered by the situations she found herself in.

Since it was my last session with her, I just gave her my recommendation that she should handle the events herself and left. I was of course interested to know how these issues had turned out because I had become very fond of her during our time together and as she said 'she had got used to me'. So when writing the book I thought it was a good opportunity to ask her how she was and if she would give me feedback on the book.

It is clear from her testimony that is on page 17 that she made the decision to trust me that these skills would work and to use the tools outlined in the book. The remark that struck me the most about what she wrote was that she was now able to build relationships which had eluded her in the past and she now realised how much she was missing out by keeping herself to herself and minding her own business. This example demonstrates how in order to develop the skills in the book, you have to believe that they will work and when you begin to believe it and apply the skills you can achieve some remarkable results.

This situation also demonstrates that as you change, events around you will shift. Some will be a reaction to you becoming more relaxed and people becoming more positive and responsive around you, Other events may be a reaction to you refusing to behave in the predictable and sometimes destructive manner you have adopted in the past.

Strangely enough I also had a similar experience of these 'shifting sands' recently so I was able to understand how my clients must feel. It was only someone helping me to unpick all the events individually (as I had done with my client) that helped me to realise that many of the adverse reactions I was experiencing were in fact the result of progress I was making in becoming more assertive in one area of my life.

Over the past 20 years I have run hundreds of assertiveness courses and am still amazed at the power that these ideas have in enabling people to identify goals and get their needs met in a healthy, direct manner. These skills will dramatically improve your interactions with others. When you have managed to get some better outcomes, you will want to continue to use and develop the skills that you have learnt.

Now that you have stabilised your interpersonal skills and gained a greater sense of control, we are ready to build on them. This is where the process of learning effective interpersonal skills becomes more enjoyable. The next stage up the continuum of interpersonal skills is influencing.

I once worked with a client who every time she raised an issue she was told to 'write a report on it'. So all her energy was taken away from the job in hand, and of course once she had written the reports, which were designed to keep her occupied and 'out of their hair', nothing happened. Until the next time she was invited to write a report.

She learnt the skills I am about to relate to you. Straight away she succeeded in getting a car park pass (these were like gold dust in her organisation). Inspired by this, she started to use influencing techniques to get people to agree to her ideas and suggestions with a minimum amount of work and a great deal of enjoyment. She even once suggested that I might be intervening in her organisation on her behalf (which I would never do), because she was achieving so many different and successful outcomes just by influencing her colleagues.

I believe that assertiveness skills underpin all the other skills on the continuum of interpersonal skills. Take your time to integrate these skills before you go onto the other skills outlined in the rest of the book.

Assertiveness

I found myself in a very confrontational situation with my boss, where I asked an executive in the organisation to intervene. On reflecting back on what was a really difficult time I realise I found the stages within assertiveness really helpful.

Before reflecting on assertiveness in the book, I would have gone in with all guns blazing and backed down when accused of overreacting or being unprofessional (my pattern when needing to be assertive previously)

Instead, I spent time beforehand working out what I wanted to achieve:

- *Recognition that certain behaviours undermined my performance and confidence in the workplace*
- *That my manager and I needed support to resolve these issues*

I described my aim and the behaviours that led me to up to taking the matter further using facts without resorting to accusation or emotive language.

So far so good, the later techniques in the book came in really helpful when I met my manager and the executive for a meeting to discuss the issues I had raised. Deflections came in thick and fast and I used "I can see why you think that way", then made a restatement of the facts … a lot…

During what was a difficult time I found the following stages (such as influencing) in the book supportive and helpful. As when my manager said "you never listen to me " I was able to ask, can you describe a particular incident and we can discuss what happened.

I was able to assert myself without resorting to aggression or sycophancy (a pattern of acting as an exploding doormat). Later

I was told that within the organisation I was seen as someone who was professional and reasonable in a less than ideal work situation.

from a client who is a Business Development Director

Reactionnaire

What are your beliefs around your ability to become more assertive when interacting with others?

What are your thoughts on the assertiveness skills that I have covered in this chapter?

What feelings did you experience as you read the information on assertiveness that was covered in this chapter?

What ideas 'popped into your head' as you read through the assertiveness skills?

What actions are you going to take as a result of reading the section on assertiveness?

Now turn to page 198, Annex 1, to explore and develop your assertiveness skills in the sample chapters from the *People Skills Revolution Companion Workbook.*
Top Tips for being more assertive: see page 181.

Chapter 6
Influencing

The Continuum of Interpersonal Skills - Influencing

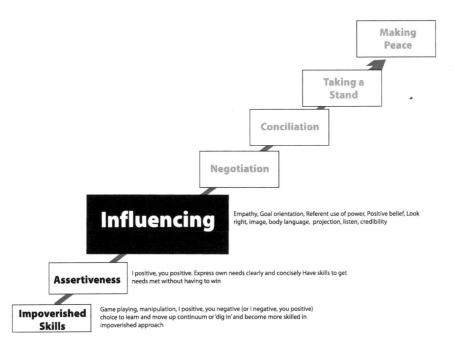

Making Peace

Taking a Stand

Conciliation

Negotiation

Influencing — Empathy, Goal orientation, Referent use of power, Positive belief, Look right, image, body language, projection, listen, credibility

Assertiveness — I positive, you positive. Express own needs clearly and concisely Have skills to get needs met without having to win

Impoverished Skills — Game playing, manipulation, I positive, you negative (or I negative, you positive) choice to learn and move up continuum or 'dig in' and become more skilled in impoverished approach

For the past 12 years I have been assisting clients to get different outcomes by using a very predictable and successful stage-by-stage model, which can be easily learnt. I have called this model 'The cycle of influence'. After learning the skills described in this chapter, people often leave a course or coaching session and achieve immediate results, after trying unsuccessfully to get things done for them by other people for many months or even years.

Being self-employed, I first developed this model when doing some 'warm calling'. In the past, before I had established my professional reputation, I had to do marketing which involved ringing people up to get them interested in the services I provide. Over the years I have found that this is easier if you have a reason to call or a previous relationship – even if it is a long time ago.

Through the grapevine, I heard that a centre director I knew 10 years previously was still in post. Since his organisation was a major purchaser of training and development, I decided to send him a brochure and marketing letter and to follow it up with a phone call.

When I rang, he took my call (which, by the way, is always a buying signal). We had a pleasant enough conversation. We talked about whether they used consultants and how much they were paid, and he promised to call me sometime. As I put the phone down, I just knew he would not call me back and felt I had managed to change a partially open door into a closed one. I wondered what had gone wrong and realised that although I had met the guy a long time ago, I had not made any attempt to build any rapport or to find out what had happened over the intervening years.

So I rang him back. Clearly, he was surprised to hear from me. I said, 'I did not just ring you up to find out if you wanted any external consultants. I wanted to chat to you, because if you are still in business after 10 years, you must be doing something right.' At this point he started talking and continued enthusiastically for the next 20 minutes. He told me how his centre was the only regional training centre left in the country, how he had to raise £2 million each year just to keep the doors open, how he had brokered an innovative Master's degree with the local university and developed a team undertaking leading-edge consultancy work. I listened and did not interrupt. When he had finished, he asked me what I had been up to.

Then I was able to tell him that I had worked for a prestigious multinational drug company, undertaken a Master's degree in Change Agent Strategies and set up my own successful consultancy, assisting organisations, people and teams with their change agendas. As I established my credibility (or why he should listen to me), he did not interrupt me. When I had finished, he simply said, 'Why don't you come and see me?'. I had achieved my goal without even trying.

When I went to see him, we had a great discussion. What I got out of that interaction was a model for influencing people, which achieves results and improves relationships between people. The model is incredibly simple. We follow the steps very naturally with people we like and feel comfortable with. For new contacts or people we do not like, it is a bit more difficult and we need to consider more consciously how we approach them.

Just think about it for a minute. You are extremely busy, and someone you like approaches you to do a favour for them. What is your response? Then someone you are not keen on or do not know asks you to do some work for them. What is your response? Since you are a human being, I assume you will say something to the person you like along the lines of, 'Well, I am incredibly busy, but since it is you, I will see what I can do'. If you have time, you will move their work up the priority list. For the person you do not know or do not have a good relationship with, you are much more likely to say, 'I am busy, so leave it there. I am doing it in order and will get around to it when I can'.

It is a well-known adage that 'people do things for people'. So if you want things to be done for you, move away from the idea that it is your role that dictates who does what for you and when. You must get to know the people you want to influence, and then present your request at a time and a pace that matches your relationship.

The cycle of influence

Following on from my 'light bulb' moment in my telephone call with the centre director above, the stages I suggest you follow are:

1. Build rapport.
2. Establish your credibility (or why they should listen to you).
3. Make your request.
4. Follow up or thank them for their assistance.

This is what I call 'The cycle of influence'.

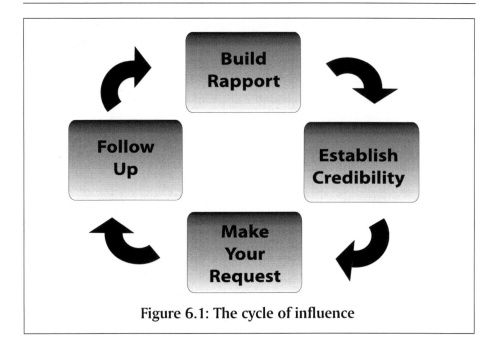

Figure 6.1: The cycle of influence

Having now used this model successfully for over 12 years, I have learnt to pace myself. Do not go onto the next stage until you are absolutely sure that you have achieved the stage before. You will find that the more you do this consciously, the more natural and unconscious it will feel. When you become really good at this, you will not even have to move it onto the next stage; the other person will do it for you by asking something like, 'You didn't just come here to ask about golf, the family or the weather. What can I do for you?'

Each of these stages requires specific skills. I am going to tell you how to develop them to achieve successful, and sometimes surprising, results.

Building rapport

Under normal circumstances, when you want to make a request for someone to do something for you and you get on well with them, you tend to have a chat with them before you ask them for what you want. Then your request flows naturally out of your conversation with them. With people you do not like or who you do not know, you often do not bother to do this.

However, taking time to get to know people or find out more about them on a personal level through building rapport and superficial conversation 'oils the wheels' of social interaction. If you only learn and apply this one skill and none of the others outlined in this book, you will find your confidence increases significantly.

Building rapport works on many levels. When done successfully, it gives you so many more choices. It enables you to walk into a room of complete strangers and be relaxed about striking up a conversation with any of them, whoever they are. It also lets you know when it is a good time to approach people and when to back off or come back later.

When it comes to making social conversation, people are all different. Some people live in a world that I might find superficial and only want to talk about football, golf, shoes or shopping. Others only relax when they feel comfortable with people. Some people think that if they are not talking about world peace, they are not having a meaningful conversation. Social conversation is a great leveller; it opens up your choices of interaction and increases your ability to build rapport and influence people substantially. If you exclude people who are not like you from your circle of influence, you will be excluding a vast proportion of the population. Given the opportunity – and approached in the right way – these people may want to get to know you better and to assist you in achieving your goals.

Another reason to be able to employ the full spectrum of conversational skills is that if you only like deep and meaningful conversation (and plenty of people do), you significantly limit the range of people and situations in which you will feel relaxed and confident. Suppose you met someone socially and you thoroughly enjoy your engagement with them at a deep level. You feel stimulated by your discussion and you look forward to seeing them another time. The problem arises when you meet that person again. It could be embarrassing and somehow inappropriate to restart the conversation where you left off. Social conversation enables you to re-engage with that person at an appropriate place, so that you can find a comfortable level for both of you again as soon as possible.

Many people are very resistant to learning to build rapport, because they dislike superficial conversation. If you are one of those, let me try to persuade you to learn this skill. If you only like meaningful conversation, you will not be able to include in your circle of influence all those people who only engage in meaningful conversation once they are relaxed with you. Equally, the people who mostly like to talk about what was on TV last night or who won the football at the weekend, just prefer to live in a more superficial world whereas you might prefer to live in a deeper one.

Two people in particular influenced my thinking on this. Both were on my courses at separate times. I noticed how they could charm other course members and get them talking. Curious and interested, I asked them how they did this. One said, 'I was a hairdresser and you just have to find a way of quickly connecting with your clients' and the other simply said, 'My mother taught me'. These replies made me realise that the charm displayed by these two people was a skill that could be learnt. I asked them what they did to build rapport. What struck me was that both of them were very conscious of using this skill. They believed that everyone had something that they really loved to talk about and the art was to find that seam of passion. So they believed that it is possible to make a connection with everyone, you just have to find that place of connection.

'Oh,' but I hear you say, ' I am just not interested in people's holidays and families and I just can't make myself appear interested.' I know you might be saying that, because I have heard the same response so many times. I used to be very much like that too, until I discovered the fascinating experience of building rapport. If you are one of those people who dislikes social conversation, the skill is to learn to love the process, not the content – to realise that it is possible to develop the skills which enable you to build that bridge between you and another person.

I believe we are social animals, living in an increasingly dehumanising society. If you do not agree with me, look at call centres or using websites or texting, instead of meeting someone face-to-face or using the phone. Given these changes in the way we interact these days, is it any wonder that when people ask us an 'off script' question about ourselves, we might hesitate to say something real and meaningful, unless we are really sure that they want to know? So you might have to try a few times to build rapport before the other person genuinely believes that you are interested in them and what they have to say.

The strange thing is that once you are able to make a connection with someone, they will find it energising to talk about things they find of interest. You may then begin to get more interested in them and what they have to say even at a superficial level.

So how do you start with building rapport? Well, find something about the person that you like or something that is worthy of comment, for example their football team, haircut, car, tie, shoes or pen and just start from there. Really, you can say just about anything, as long as it is not important or serious – you are simply giving out the signal that you are open for conversation. Then ask a couple of questions about the person, and if they respond well, you might like to introduce yourself. Unless you are just practising at a bus stop, see it as a long-term goal, not a one-off conversation. Build on anything that you have found out about the person the next time you meet them.

Also, be prepared to give other people what is called 'free information' about yourself in order to build rapport, otherwise it can feel very one-sided. Free information should include those topics of conversation, which you are comfortable sharing with others. Make a list of things you like to talk about socially and chat about them when encouraged to do so by others. We all have hidden shallows, and building rapport is both a time to discover the other person's and to reveal yours. One of my clients uses a mug with his football team's logo on it. It does not take much imagination to work out how many superficial – or even not so superficial – conversations that this small rapport-building device has started.

Here is another example of building rapport in a real situation. I was running a course and a participant walked in. It was clear that she was very angry. Before coming into the training room, she perceived that a work colleague had been rude to her on the phone. Throughout the workshop she interspersed all her comments with: 'I think I deserve an apology. Don't you think I deserve an apology?'. By the afternoon break she was still annoyed and was still going on about wanting an apology. Although I explained the power of building rapport during the workshop, she was so preoccupied with her thoughts that I did not imagine that she had even been listening.

During the afternoon break, she went down to the department and started building rapport with the woman concerned. She said she found it incredibly difficult because of her anger, and was annoyed because she had to listen to the woman talking about her cold and how ill she felt. After she had listened to her for about 10 minutes, the woman turned to her and said, 'I am so sorry for snapping at you earlier, I just was not feeling well'. She had achieved her apology without really trying. If she had tackled the problem head on from an angry position, it is likely that she would have made the situation worse.

Of course, some people are notoriously difficult to get to know, so respect their boundaries and develop your skills with other people before approaching them. Remember, though, that these people may keep everyone at a distance and may feel very isolated. If you do try to build rapport with them, do it in a way that suits them and take your time. They may be particularly appreciative of your efforts – even though they may not show it immediately.

This is what one client, a director of finance, said about what her new ability to build rapport means to her.

'Walking into a room of strangers and being comfortable to speak. I had to attend a conference dinner with an arranged

seating plan. I was put on one of the top tables and not sitting next to my colleague. I knew I would have to actively engage in conversation with senior executives. I would normally shy away from this situation – doing anything to avoid it. Having used the techniques to build rapport, which I am still learning, I felt confident initiating conversation. After formal instructions, using the specific technique of having a 'conversation piece' – 'rapport building device'; to use as a topic of conversation, I use my complicated, difficult to pronounce surname as a starting point – as a focus to break into informal conversation. This then set me on a journey of increasing confidence to have normal conversation with those whom I would normally perceive to be 'out of my league' professionally. Through this encounter I was able to make contacts to use in the future.

This also helps me feel, I'm in control of a conversation at work because I can then make the judgment when it is a suitable point to bring up more 'heavy' topics or approach a difficult conversation'.

Psychological types

When building rapport, there is another factor that you might want to consider: how people communicate in very different ways. This was demonstrated by the research of the psychologist Carl Jung, who, having worked with thousands of clients, noticed patterns in the way that people communicate. In 1921 he published a book called *Psychological Types*[2], in which he identified four dominant communication types:

- intuitor
- thinker
- feeler
- sensor.

I will explain what the descriptions mean in more detail below. First I would like to say something about this model.

2   Princeton University Press (Revised edition 1976)

The intuitor, thinker, feeler, sensor categories are a great way of understanding how we interpret events and of understanding how or why others might interpret events very differently. Although most of us have a primary orientation in terms of our communication styles, we also have the other three styles and abilities within us. It just depends what order we tend to do things and how strong our preference is for each style. We can usually use the point of similarity to make a connection with another person.

As a rule, we tend to get on easily with people who are like us and have a similar style, and to be perplexed by people who are very different from us. If you have ever met someone and had an immediate rapport with them and felt as though you have known them for a very long time, it is usually because you have very similar communication styles. On the other hand, if you meet someone and communication is very stilted or you lack a point of connection, you may at times wonder if they live on the same planet as you. Their approach can be so different from our own that we simply do not know how to communicate with them – it is as if we are having parallel conversations that do not overlap.

Occasionally, nothing we try to do to build bridges or make things better with some people has any impact. It can even make it worse. This is where this model is particularly useful. The four psychological types explain why people may do things in a certain way, which can be illogical or even irritating to us. We wonder why they are doing a task in a particular way and it may cross our mind that they are being 'difficult' on purpose.

Learning about these styles helps us to understand ourselves better and also to adapt our style to communicate more effectively with others. Below I outline how intuitors, thinkers, feelers and sensors tend to view the world. Consider which of the four communication styles might be dominant for you – and for your boss, colleagues, friends, partner, or family members.

You can tell which might be your preferred style by your reactions to the explanations. If you are drawn to the descriptions of one style, it is likely that you have a large part of that style in your personality. If you find yourself reacting against any of the descriptions, the chances are that this approach is the least dominant (and least favoured) style in your personality.

To bring the four types to life, at the end of each description I have outlined what kind of occupations each group is attracted to and illustrated how they would approach a typical work project, using the example of arranging an office move. I then suggest how you would use knowledge of the model to build rapport with each of the personality types.

Intuitor

Intuitors are people with lots of ideas, creativity and originality. They live in the future and are always coming up with new plans and possibilities. They like change and as soon as things become routine, they get bored.

Their communication style is loose and unstructured. Talking to them can be like trying to catch a butterfly – you just think you have caught them and then they fly off in another direction. People who have a tendency to be intuitors often find jobs which require creativity. Intuitors are attracted to being inventors, planners, artists, scientists, researchers or advertising executives.

Their time sense is the future. If planning an office move, intuitors would consider new technology, suggest innovative working practices like 'hot desking', source high design furniture and create an environment where creativity and discussion could flourish. On the downside, they would not always consider the cost implications of their plans nor pay attention to important details or deadlines.

If they find themselves in organisational cultures that are very different from how they like to work (like banking, production and the health service), they may not fit in very easily and may be considered to be a bit 'off the wall'.

If you want to build rapport and communicate effectively with an intuitor, try to get into their world, talk about new ideas or innovations. Discuss philosophical concepts and ideas or ask them for suggestions to improve systems or even society.

Thinker

Thinkers are organised, logical, systematic, precise and analytical. They like to make plans and to know where everything is. Before making a decision, they like to undertake research and compare options. They cannot quite understand why other people are not more like them or why they would want to surround themselves with clutter. In their eyes, having a place for everything and everything in its place is the key to having an organised life and reducing stress. They like developing systems and producing reports and documents. They also appreciate having all of the information they need to hand and prefer not to go to meetings if they have not thoroughly prepared for what is likely to be discussed.

Their time sense is the past, present and future, and they will consider any information that is relevant to a particular project. If planning an office move, thinkers would have lists and charts for all eventualities. At any given time they would be able to tell you precisely where you are in the process.

If you are trying to sell an idea or concept to them, it can be quite frustrating if you are not another thinker. Because they like so many facts and figures, even if you think that you have researched and discussed every possible aspect of a situation, they will ask you yet another question to clarify a point. Thinkers will agree that it can take them a long time to make a decision, but when they have made it, they will be completely confident that they have made the right decision.

They can also get irritated with changes that occur and are not usually considered to be the most flexible of the styles.

Their communication style reflects their outlook on life. They are very organised and thorough in the way they present information. Because of their very systematic and logical nature, they tend to go into jobs like accountancy, information technology, science and the legal profession.

If you want to build rapport with a thinker, it can be quite difficult. They may often be impatient with social conversation and feel that it wastes time. So be very professional in your approach. Discuss business first, then gradually move on to relevant social or superficial conversation. If they are busy, come back later at an agreed time, when they are a bit more relaxed.

Feeler

Feelers work a lot on their instinct and gut reaction. They can walk into a room and sense an atmosphere. Their primary orientation to the world is people and they love to take time out to have a coffee and a chat. Other people would see this as gossiping, but a feeler will often regard it as networking. A feeler is likely to know most about what is happening in a workplace, group setting or family. They can make decisions based on emotional reactions or factors that others would find illogical.

The time sense of the feeler is the past. If planning an office move, a feeler would take into account the personal dynamics between the people and would consider who should be positioned next to each other. To other styles this might appear to be unnecessary or appear to be oversensitive, but a feeler would consider this vital to avoid the disruptions that happened during the previous reorganisation.

Because of their focus on people, those with a feeler tendency are attracted to jobs in healthcare, sales, teaching, public relations and human resources.

Building rapport with a person who is a feeler is easy. Just smile, pull up a chair, and offer them a drink. Then ask them what they did over the weekend or anything that will get them talking.

Sensor

Sensors are action-orientated, quick-thinking, technically skilled and decisive. They like to get things done with a minimum of fuss and get impatient with detail, impractical ideas, feelings and long explanations. They judge the success of their day on how much they have achieved and get frustrated with people who are not as quick-thinking or fast-acting as they are.

Sensors look as though they are not basing their quick decision-making on anything, but their main skill is in rapidly weighing up a number of factors simultaneously. Although they do not like to dissect their thinking process in this way, when pushed they can explain why they made a particular decision.

The time sense of the sensor is now. If planning an office move, the main factor they would consider is, 'Are we on track or not?' The downside to this approach is that the other styles would consider that they have not fully explored all the factors that need to be considered. Sensors can also come across as impatient.

Because their style is so different, there can be friction between sensors and the other styles. Sensors need to become more tolerant of people and to realise that other people have different and apparently slower processes than they do. They also need to take the time to learn the language of the other styles and consider how they can present their ideas in a range of styles.

In turn, the other styles need to present information more succinctly to the sensor. They should only tell them the key facts or headlines and be able to suggest solutions to any problems that they present. If you are able to do this, you will find that sensor-type people start to listen to you and respect your opinion – almost as though they have heard you for the first time.

Due to their action orientation they tend to go into jobs like engineering, production, surgeon, account manager or sales executive.

In terms of rapport-building, keep it short, relevant and interesting. Don't ramble or be tangential, and do it in the short spaces between the action, when they might enjoy a bit of light distraction.

Due to their action tendency, sensors can be promoted before they are ready. They can also have very short fuses when they show their impatience with another style. On the positive side, they bring vital drive and energy to organisational life. With a very few simple shifts, both sensors and the other styles can learn to communicate more effectively.

When using this approach you have to trade off the idea of being understood – for being heard. A sensor is never going to understand why a feeler is upset, unless they have feeler as their own personal back-up style; but a feeler can learn to present their ideas in such a way that the sensor will understand the issues and agree to the actions that they suggest. Given the choice between being heard or understood, most of us would choose to be heard and to have our ideas lead to action.

I am a feeler/intuitor. Years ago, I used to work for a boss who was off the scale in terms of being a thinker. His desk was always tidy, and as far as I could see, so was his mind. Every time I went into his office with my ideas and feelings, I could see him looking at me as if I were a Martian. The more he failed to understand what I was saying, the more frustrated I became. After nearly all our conversations he would look at me totally bemused and say, 'So what do you want me to do about it?'. In my appraisals he called me oversensitive. When I heard this, I was screaming to myself inside my head, 'Oversensitive? At least I have feelings! I could be slumped over a desk with a dagger in my back and you wouldn't notice!' Then it suddenly occurred to me that when he said 'What do you want me to do about it?', that is what he meant. Instead of going into his office ready for a confrontation, I went in with a plan. After leading him logically through my idea (in a very A to B, C to D kind of way), almost like magic he started to say yes to my ideas. The ideas had not changed; my feelings had not changed. I had simply learnt to present them in a way that he could hear.

When people first hear about this model, many of them say, 'So does this mean that we need to start analysing everyone we come into contact with?'. The simple answer is no. Most interactions are just fine and cause you no difficulty. This approach comes in useful in situations where you just do not get on and no matter how hard you try, the situation seems to get worse between you. This is usually a very good indicator of a clash in styles and suggests a need to use this model to diagnose the problem and change the way you are interacting with the other person.

Jung's concept of communication styles can lead to some 'light bulb' moments. When running a management course, I shared this model with the participants and five months later, when the course ended, one man said that the approach had saved his marriage, since he now understood why he and his wife were so different. Using the ideas presented, he had found strategies to talk to her so that the communication between them had improved significantly. Another participant said it had helped him to understand why there was such a poor 'fit' between his work style and the work style of the organisation he was working in. This is because certain styles are attracted to certain types of occupations due to the nature of the job and the requirement to work in a certain way.

You can also use knowledge of the four styles to prepare for presentations, write reports and 'sell' your ideas to managers, friends and families. If you can learn to adapt your style to the needs of others, people will appreciate your efforts, and the relationship and your ability to build rapport with them will improve substantially as a result.

Establishing credibility

When you have managed to improve your ability to built rapport in content, style and approach, it is likely that the person you are talking to will say the equivalent of: 'You have not just come here to chat to me about my interest in sailing. What do you want?' When asked such a direct question, it is very tempting to then tell them what you want, but resist doing this at this stage. Before you tell people what you want, establish your credibility with them, or in other words, explain to them why they should listen to you. This stage will substantially increase the likelihood of getting your requests accepted and acted upon.

People who establish their credibility in the eyes of the people they want to influence substantially increase their chances of getting their needs met.

This is how I learnt this lesson. When I first started running training programmes, it felt as though I was 'pushing a boulder up a hill' until about 11am. Just before the morning break I could almost see the delegates start to smile, relax and decide that it was all right to be on the course. This felt like incredibly hard work for me. I also expect that the participants would have preferred to know at the outset that the course was going to be useful to them and that they would both benefit from it and enjoy it. In fact, it had become such hard work that I was considering giving up training people, and I had gone into a negative downward spiral about my skills.

At this point I went to be assessed as a potential candidate for a leading national process consultancy, but because I did not have the skills to build rapport or 'sell myself', I felt very uncomfortable. At the end of the assessment day, the facilitator told me that they had decided not to take my application forward but at the same time gave me some feedback that changed my working and personal life. He said: 'You **are** very good, but you take a long time to warm up'. Immediately he said this, it struck a chord. I realised that I was not establishing my credibility with people – I was just allowing it to emerge as I was working.

As a result of this feedback, I make a point of establishing my credibility and letting participants know why they should listen to me at the beginning of each course. Depending on the group and the level I am working at, I explain that I have a background in their industry, let them know I have a Master's degree in Change Agent Skills and Strategies and, if relevant, share with them that I have been through a similarly difficult time to them. I might also tell them that I have been a manager, that I have worked with prestigious corporate clients and suggest that I like their organisation and respect what it does. I tell them that I have used the skills I am going to share with them to help me, and thousands of others, to achieve some dramatically different outcomes. I do this in a very upbeat manner, with a warm smile and the odd touch of humour.

Of course, my spiel varies considerably depending on the group or person I am working with, but I always ask myself 'How will I get their attention and how will I get them listening to me?'. Now I find that I generally have their engagement right from the beginning of a course.

Successful people establish their credibility constantly, when they realise that there is a need to do so. So it is a good habit to get into, especially when you notice that for some reason a person or group is not taking you as seriously as you would like them to. This practice is not about 'blowing your own trumpet', although many people feel that it is. It is simply laying the foundations in terms of your background, experience and expertise to highlight why they should listen to you.

People are influenced by people who they consider to be equal to them. If you learn these skills, it will help to shift the balance of relationships from 'I negative, you positive' to 'I positive, you positive' for whoever you are working with.

On one of my courses, I was talking to a very able clinical governance professional, who said that whenever she talked to medical consultants, they would do the equivalent of patting her on the head, saying 'There, there, young lady, we will deal with this' – and they dealt with it in their own style and timeframe. After she used these techniques, she managed to shift the balance of power to a more equal footing. When I next bumped into her, she said that they were now treating her as a fellow colleague and they were working together to build and deliver the governance strategy.

Most people do not find it easy to talk about themselves positively and to tell people about their background and the skills they bring. It seems to take them way out of their comfort zone. Learning to do this with style is the key to coming across as confident but without appearing arrogant.

I spend a significant part of my working life (as a company director) preparing and presenting complex and often unwelcome information/ideas to disparate groups of people.

In terms of influencing: learning how to "establish credibility" has been a valuable and now always used skill in my tool box.

Before I would prepare my information carefully, rehearse what I was going to say and then go in and attempt to dazzle them with the content of my presentation or contribution at a meeting.

Now I answer the first two questions that pre-exist in a listeners head:

- *what am I going to be doing here*
- *who is he?*

So in response I open with a brief description of what is going to happen/happened and then describe my previous positive experience using a process of:

- *describing a challenge*
- *the action I took to overcome*
- *the resulting success story.*

I keep everything short and snappy. If people are going to buy my ideas or engage with the information I present they have to believe in me and once I have them on board then I can launch into the presentation/meeting.

Only recently I turned around a poor performing team and enabled them to improve on their performance targets. To do so I invested time establishing my credibility and this paid off with high praise from the CEO of the organisation.

Sources of power

One way to reflect on what you can say to establish credibility is to consider the concept of sources of power. We all have power, whether or not we choose to use it. This exercise will get you reacquainted with yours.

If you want to increase or establish your credibility, become more familiar with your sources of power. Some typical headings for power sources are:

- **legitimate** – from your position in an organisation or your legal role
- **referent** – from your personality – qualities that you have which people remember, for example your approachability or your smile
- **information** – from your knowledge base
- **expert** – from your expertise and skills
- **reward** – from what you can offer people in relation to their needs
- **coercive** – from your ability to make people do things that they do not want to do.

Jot down some notes against each of these headings and keep on coming back to them, until you think you have a complete and clear picture of what you bring to a situation. Consider your knowledge, background, skills, experience and temperament. A good clue to your areas of expertise is to think of the times when people come to you for advice, rather than going to a colleague. An indication of your reward power is what you can do for people when they have done an especially good job for you, for example putting them on a course that might be beneficial to them or giving them a particular task that you know they will enjoy. Although I would not suggest that you get good at using your coercive power, it is important to realise that you do have it and that it can be used appropriately when necessary for example to call security if a situation gets out of hand or to use company policies and procedures where necessary.

Adapt what you share with the people you are trying to influence according to what they might be interested to know about you. Although I have found that most people feel highly uncomfortable selling themselves, if you want to influence someone around to your point of view, you have to establish your credibility with them first. This is no time to be bashful.

Your sources of power

What are your legitimate sources of power?

What are your referent sources of power?

What information do you have access to that gives you power?

What expertise do you have that gives you power?

What rewards can you offer people in relation to their needs that would give you power?

And finally what coercive power do you have to make people do things that they do not want to do?

Influential people do not just establish their credibility when they first meet a new person or group; they do it at any point when they need to increase their impact and remind people why they should listen to them.

The hierarchy of language

Building rapport and establishing credibility is also about understanding the natural agendas that people have due to their hierarchical position in a group – whether it is a large organisation, a small company or a family.

Put simply, this means that whatever the individual styles or motivations of a person, they will have agendas allocated to their roles. These agendas are defined by the role itself, and by where the roles are in the hierarchy. This process of shifting agendas happens quite subconsciously, even when people are not intending this to happen.

I developed this approach when working with a group of newly appointed care managers. They were clearly perplexed to find themselves saying phrases to staff that they had insisted they would never use if they got promoted from their previous positions as support workers. Now, they kept hearing themselves using exactly the same kind of language that their managers used to say to them. If you are a parent, this may sound familiar.

The simple reason for this shift in language is that although you have not changed, the role itself decides your agenda and the concerns you will be interested in hearing about.

For the sake of simplicity, I have labelled the levels of the organisational hierarchy as 'On the shop floor', 'Supervisor', 'Manager' and 'Strategist' (see Figure 6.2). This model will help you to understand what agendas might be uppermost in your mind in your current role, when you consider a particular topic or event. You can then use the model to enable you to understand how the same topic or event might be interpreted through the agendas of other people in terms of their positions within the organisational hierarchy. If you want to influence someone towards your point of view, you must frame your comments in the light of their agendas, rather than the agendas that might be of most interest to you.

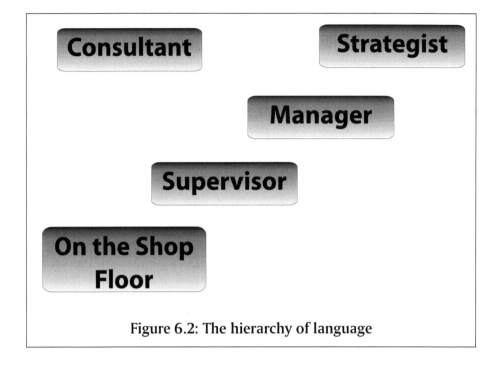

Figure 6.2: The hierarchy of language

Agendas at each level of the hierarchy

If you are working directly with clients 'On the shop floor', your concerns will be:

- the quality of the service you are providing
- the resources you have available to you
- any operational issues and difficulties
- getting the job done and doing it well
- your own personal safety and the safety of the people you work with and for.

If you are a supervisor, your major concerns will be:

- achieving targets and deadlines
- getting the goods out of the door
- minimising complaints
- working within available resources
- finding solutions to problems
- achieving safe working practices.

If you are a manager, your concerns and agenda shift again. They will be:

- introducing change
- concern for the customers as a group
- improving systems and procedures
- limiting expenditure and reducing cost
- implementing strategic initiatives
- advocating a case for additional resources
- developing health and safety policies and procedures.

If you are a strategist, your agendas and concerns will be:

- competition with other similar organisations
- managing the relationship with shareholders and internal/external stakeholders
- meeting financial performance targets to increase profit or stay within budget
- establishing organisational goals/targets
- projecting a positive image of the organisation
- corporate responsibility for health and safety.

This strategist agenda explains why you could be working in an organisation that you may consider to be poorly run and inefficient, but when you read the press releases, it paints a wonderfully positive image. This is the nature of the role. If you want to influence a strategist, tell them something that would help them to improve the promotion of the service or business or help them to avoid receiving criticism from stakeholders and shareholders.

If there are senior people within the organisation who are not part of the management structure, for example consultants on a major project, this group will also have their own language agendas.

The agendas of the consultant will be:

- influencing the management structure
- the quality of the service
- sufficiency of resources
- their status in relation to others
- their self-image
- hidden agendas
- safety of procedures.

A member of staff was heard complaining to a secretary that she had not been able to get a consultant to engage with her project. The secretary kept on typing, turned her head and said matter-of-factly: 'Have you tried flattery?'. While you may recoil at the thought of using flattery to get your ideas considered, would you rather be heard or ignored?

The way to use these agendas at each level of the organisation is to realise that if you present your arguments in the language of their interests rather than your own, you will substantially increase your chances of getting your views accepted. This is not an easy skill to learn, but once you develop this technique, your influencing skills will be enhanced significantly.

Let me give you a few examples to bring the concept of the language of hierarchical agendas to life.

When mobile phones first came out, they were very expensive and so was the cost of calls. As a result, parents were wary about buying them for their children. At the time, I overheard concerned parents in mobile phone shops saying to their teenage daughters, 'Now, you do realise that this is just for emergency use, don't you?'. The young person would look on solemnly and nod. This illustrates that the teenagers had learnt it would be pointless telling their parents that they wanted to use the phone to chat with their friends. Instead, they realised that the safety and protection of children is clearly very prominent on the parental agenda. It was far easier and more effective to 'sell' the mobile phone purchase to the parents as a safety measure. Both agendas are realistic from each person's perspective, but selling the safety agenda got the parents ready to buy the phone, whereas the teenager's perspective would most likely have been discounted.

When employed in an organisation, I used this concept of selling a different perspective with my boss. I wanted to undertake a Master's degree but knew that three of my colleagues had already been allowed to study for Master's degrees that year. When planning my response to his probable objections, I realised that the 'But that's not fair' comment was not likely to impress him. So I considered his agenda. He needed to be seen to be delivering a professional service, improving the image of his department and to be respected by his manager and colleagues. So when he did object, instead of playing the 'fairness' card, which would not have influenced him, I told him that if he supported my application, he would be seen to running a service where all of his team were operating at Master's degree level. I then suggested that this would add a lot of kudos to our department. Immediately, I could see him thinking 'Yes, I could argue that, if I was challenged about my decision'.

To give another example, I was explaining this model to a group and a delegate became agitated and said to me, 'I had a care assistant come up to me and say, there is a cola bottle in the drug fridge'. He said, 'What am I supposed to do about that?'. I said to delegate, 'But what if she had come up to you and told you that there was a cola bottle in the drug fridge which created a risk of contamination, and if the drugs were damaged in any way it would jeopardise thousands of pounds of supplies, would you have been more interested?'. He responded, 'Yes of course, but she did not say that'.

The point in all these examples is that the information is exactly the same, but the way the information is packaged, in relation to the agenda of the person they wanted to influence, is different. So if you want to sell an idea to a boss, colleague, senior manager or even a family member, consider their agenda. Think about how you can present your ideas to be of interest to them, and also consider how they would sell the idea upwards to their superiors.

Making a shift in language to reflect the other person's role in the organisation is not an easy concept to explain. It can also be difficult to understand. Just remember that if you state your ideas in terms of your own role agenda, you are less likely to be listened to; if you state your ideas in terms of the other person's role agenda, you are much more likely to be able to get onto their wavelength. Your message will come across much more clearly, and you will significantly increase your chances of getting your ideas heard and adopted.

New ideas can often stimulate a lot more work for the people who have to make the decision to adopt them. Since most people are averse to effort, when it comes to taking on additional work, try to do some of the thinking and processing for them. It is amazing how an irritating whine from a subordinate which sounds like self-interest can be transformed into a positive and welcomed suggestion, by considering the agenda of the person you want to influence.

Incidentally, I ran the course for the care managers in 1994 when I first became an independent consultant. When I was writing this book I attended a meditation seminar. At events like this it is rare to stray into what you do for a living, but on this occasion we did. The woman I was talking to told me that she now worked in accountancy and finance but had spent most of her career in the care sector. As soon as she said that I realised that she was one of the three people I had trained on the course that stimulated the development of the hierarchy of language model. She then told me that the organisation had recognised her skills and that she had been 'allowed to fly' resulting in her running the organisation. As a group the three course members also went on to became the top performing managers in the company and had been able to successfully navigate through the changes brought about through legislation that the course had been designed to facilitate.

Making a request

You should now be able to build rapport and establish your credibility with the person you want to influence. You will have done this by considering their interests and communication style and adapting your language to match the agenda of their role within the organisational structure. If you have presented your ideas in a style and content that is of relevance to the other party, you will have managed to get their attention. They are now probably wondering why you have approached them in this way.

If you wait long enough, their curiosity will get the better of them and they will say something like, 'You have not just come to see me to have a chat and tell me what you have been up to over the past few weeks. What do you want?' When you hear this, you know that they are ready for your intervention. Since you have taken the time to get to know them and have outlined your issues in relation to their agenda, you will have considerably increased your chances of getting a successful outcome.

It is much harder to say no to someone when you have just spent the last few minutes chatting with them. After you have been talking to them for a while to build rapport and establish your credibility, you are likely to get the opportunity to make the request that you have been looking for. The other person will either ask you directly 'What do you want?' or a space will appear for you to ask your question. Then state what you want to happen, simply and clearly. If the timing still does not feel right, back off. Maybe you need to increase your rapport with them, or perhaps you have not quite established your credibility in their eyes. Leave your request until you think that the time is right for you to ask.

Following up and saying thanks

Managing to influence someone around to your point of view is not the end of the story. Follow up your interaction with them. In the process of talking, if you have agreed to do something for them, you must do it. If they do something for you, you must thank them. Do what you promise to do and thank people for doing what they do for you. This creates goodwill, which will enable you to continue building the relationship the next time you meet them. It also prevents people from feeling that they have been manipulated.

More often than not these days a 'thank you' is treated as a precious and rare commodity to be used only in the most exceptional circumstances. Saying 'thank you' and providing information that is useful to the other party costs nothing, takes no time at all and creates an 'economy of thanks and goodwill'. This 'economy of thanks', will stand you in good stead on an interaction-to-interaction basis. It will also support your ability to influence and network throughout your career. Saying thank you and appreciating the efforts of others is also infectious. The more 'thank yous' you say, the more you increase your likelihood of receiving 'thank yous' back – and these will not necessarily come from the people you said 'thank you' to in the first place.

At Follow Up stage it is important to be clear if you are trying to influence over the long term or trying to sell. Influencing is about building a lasting relationship and taking it slowly. It is about thanking them for their time, making an observation about the interaction you had with them and keeping the door open for further contact – not making another request or asking for more. At this point people do not want to read anything too detailed or technical. Keep it simple so that the other person does not have to think about it and can quickly register your appreciation. One way to do this is to imagine yourself talking to them and use similar language when thanking them in writing.

Now you are probably thinking that you are busy enough, without having to take the time to influence someone. You might even resent doing it. Instead of seeing influencing as taking up time, regard it as investment. Time spent at this stage will prevent problems from occurring later on in the project. Generally speaking, influencing someone at the outset smooths the whole process and improves your working relationships in the longer term.

Influencing people is enjoyable for you and the people you influence. If you do it with style, you will start to achieve goals you never before thought possible.

If you have learnt to influence, it is likely that you will be wondering how you can use your skills to get a new job or increase your profile within an organisation or group. Most people believe that if they work hard, this will lead to excellent feedback and promotion. They are then bemused when people with less experience and skills get promoted over them. In his book *Empowering Yourself – The Organizational Game Revealed*[3], Harvey Coleman explains that there are three factors which lead to people getting recognition. These are performance, visibility and image. So far, so good. What is surprising, are the proportions of the relevant percentages, in terms of importance, for each of these factors. Coleman found that 60% of recognition could be put down to visibility – being known around the organisation or group. Some 30% can be attributed to image – how we present ourselves to others in terms of our dress, manner and body language. The more shocking statistic is that only about

---

3   Kendall/Hunt Publishing Company 1996

10% of recognition can be put down to performance – what we actually achieve in our jobs.

When I share this research with people on my programmes, there is a stunned silence. A few minutes later I hear rumblings of 'But that's not fair'. Well, it may not be fair, but this research is played out in most people's experience.

Here I cannot resist telling a story. I once worked for an organisation where we more or less did no work. When people rang up to use our service, my boss would tell them we were too busy. We were based next to a park and the secretary and I used to fantasise about opening a sandwich bar. The milkman became a frequent visitor and would often sit in the office, playing his guitar. The whole place was a bit unusual. But, my boss was well liked and people always believed that he was very busy, which was a mystery to us. One day he went up to the headquarters on his daily visit and asked me if I wanted to go with him. When we got there, he systematically went into all the offices. Although he appeared to be in a hurry to be elsewhere, he took the time to say hello to everyone and made social conversation with them. When he had been into every office, and had had a pleasant chat, he got into his car and left, leaving everyone to think that he was always very pleasant despite his busyness. He was a master at managing his visibility and his image.

So, rather than working hard, keeping your head down and hoping that someone will notice you, pay attention to how you are perceived within your organisation. One very effective way of increasing your influence is to take the time to have chats with people.

The power of chats

If I work with people for any length of time, it is not long before I start talking about the power of chats. I am a huge believer in just chatting with people. By this, I mean not making a big thing about making an appointment to meet people. This can make everything so serious. Instead, take the time to have coffee with people, meet people for lunch, bump into them in the corridor, talk over the photocopier and build up relationships just for the sake of it.

This is an approach that has certainly paid off in my work. Many of the ideas in this book were brought to life, polished or transformed when talking to clients, colleagues or friends. Using chats, I have over the years been able to secure a great deal of repeat business and have been invited to undertake assignments with an increasing level of complexity. In my dealings with clients, I always try to initiate low-key meetings, keep people 'in the loop', deliver on agreements and be friendly, visible and professional. During these meetings I very rarely talk about business, unless they initiate it. My aim is get to know the client as a person, and if I can help them with any aspect of their business or their personal agenda without actually taking on unpaid work I will do this. As a result, I have assisted them with their CVs, suggested books that they might like to read and inspired them to go for jobs that they might not otherwise have considered. Additional work has also often resulted from these meetings, sometimes when I least expected it. If they leave the organisation, I am often able to retain their previous organisation as a client, while still working with the former client in his or her new organisation.

For me, magic occurs when I have chats with people. I find information I need, and people who I want (or need) to talk to are recommended to me. This happens for the other person too. This is a subtle process that emerges as you chat to people. Do not try to force it, but allow it to unravel. Some people would call this networking, and of course that is part of it. But it is much more than that. This is about putting the skills of influencing into play, but with a light touch. When influencing and networking with people, take your time to build rapport, be prepared to establish your credibility and make sure that when you meet someone, you treat them as a person, not as a vehicle to do something for you.

In other words you are projecting a positive image of yourself and you are taking the time and trouble to be visible within an organisation. If you do this, you will be much more likely to be the person they think of when the next promotion is due or when the next big project comes up. If you think about it, you could be the best singer, artist, writer or manager in the world, but if no one knows about you, what is the point? Given the choice between the indispensable departmental 'work horse', the argumentative prima donna or the professional and reliable person who visible, presentable and easy to work with, who would you choose?

To assist you further in your chatting, I want to tell you how to become a better listener and a better questioner.

How to become a better listener

A few years ago, one of my clients asked me to run a coaching skills workshop. This was a very interesting challenge for me. Although I had been a coach for many years by then, and had a very successful track record, I had never actually learnt how to coach.

My career as an executive coach began in 2002 when business coaching was in its infancy. A client wanted to set up an innovative coaching programme within her organisation and asked me if I had any experience of coaching. I said that I had done a lot of outplacement which is about getting people quickly from one job to another and she said 'that will do'.

So building on the experience I had already gained when working with people in transition during times of change in the workplace I became an executive coach.

I will never forget my first two-hour coaching session. I spent the first 40 minutes listening to him and thinking to myself, 'This cannot be right, there must be more to it than this'. Then he stopped and said, 'Do you know, this is really good?'. It was at that point that I realised the incredible power of a listening ear.

After I had written this book, I met up with this client socially and told him about this anecdote He laughed out loud and told me his side of the story. He was amazed that it was my first, ever coaching session and had gone home to his partner and told her that he had a 'shit hot' coach. According to the Urban Dictionary this term means 'outstanding, incredible, above expectations, motivating', which cannot be bad for a two hour session. I think this story does demonstrate the power of listening.

During this session and all the subsequent coaching sessions, I realised that coaching, or in fact, any effective interpersonal interaction, is underpinned by listening and questioning. This presented me with a challenge – how do you teach someone to become a better listener and questioner?

I came across a very useful idea in *The Coaching Manual* by Julie Starr[4] that listening skills could be divided into four levels:

- cosmetic
- conversational
- active
- deep.

This concept helps people to understand that listening at each of these levels can have a different impact and requires different skills. Since these skills are cumulative, Starr refers to it as a hierarchy of listening skills. You should not go on to the next level of skills before you have mastered the skills at the previous level.

Cosmetic listening

At the cosmetic level, you are not really listening at all. Although you are physically present, you might be thinking about who else is around who might be more interesting or more attractive to talk to. You might also be thinking about what you are having for dinner or your journey home. Only the most unaware people will

---

4   Prentice Hall Business 2010

think that they are having a real conversation. It is also true that there a quite a few unaware people around.

Conversational listening

At the conversational level, you are both engaging with each other. I visualise this like playing tennis. You lob a comment over the net and they lob one back. If we are honest, at this level we are thinking about what we want to say next before they have finished talking. We are concentrating on finding a space to slot our comment into. Here the quality of the interaction is much better than at the cosmetic level of listening. It is also usually much more enjoyable, although it can also be frustrating and competitive for people, as they try to get their views heard.

Active listening

The next level in the hierarchy is active listening. This is when the attention of the listener is firmly on the talker. When I am coaching, this is where I work most of the time. I tend to just listen and make notes as I go, looking for patterns or themes in what the person is saying. This model made me realise that improving listening skills is just a decision that we can all make when we choose to put the other person's agenda above our own. We may do this in order to assist them to understand the issues that they are dealing with or to help us understand their perspective.

Although active listening can be incredibly tiring if done for more than a couple of hours at a time, it can enable the talker to learn a lot about themselves and about people with whom they interact. Active listening can also make it an extremely rewarding experience for the coach. I cannot tell you the number of times in a coaching session that, after listening to a series of events, I have come up with an insightful comment or suggestion for the client's benefit that has later been useful to me in my own life.

Let me give you an example of the benefits of active listening. I was once working with a senior manager who was new to the post. During the conversation she was telling me that she had had a number of disagreements with people in the various departments under her charge. If I had not been actively listening, I might have interrupted her after each description of an incident and explored what might have happened in each case. Instead I decided to keep quiet and let her story unravel. After she had finished talking, it occurred to me that it was too much of a pattern to be a pure accident. I reflected for a moment and said, 'It strikes me that they think that you are interfering'. At this point, her head went down and her shoulders slumped and she said, 'That's why I left my last job'. The focus of our discussion then moved away from each incident towards helping her to address and reduce her need to control.

I have also found something else interesting at this level. If you listen hard and summarise what people have said to you – often using their own words – and say something like, 'So what you are saying is …', people will usually say 'Yes, yes, that's it. You are exactly right.' Occasionally they used to stump me by saying 'No, that's not what I think at all'. This took me by surprise, since I was sure I was listening hard and in fact using their own words. Then I became curious and began to ask them 'Well, if it is not that, what is it?'. To my surprise, they often had a fully worked out alternative view all ready and waiting in the background. While it is hard to say why this may be the case, my guess would be that our ideas and perspectives take a while to change and maybe we have to have our views reflected back to us before we can decide to adopt our new perspectives. In this instance, our listening would still be valuable, but instead of promoting reflection and integration, it would be catalytic – changing an experience from one state to another. I think these conversations can be pivotal to help people understand how they see the world and how they can change this view.

Becoming an active listener has many benefits for both parties. To achieve this, you simply need to make the decision to focus your attention on the other person. When you become an active listener, you will hear more of what people are saying, but maybe most importantly, you also start to notice what they are not saying. People communicate their ideas and views unconsciously without often realising it. I believe that people know most of the answers to their own questions – they just do not know they know. Allowing people to talk while you listen, often allows their own answers to be revealed to them.

Deep listening

Becoming a deep listener is somewhat more complicated. Deep listening is when you unconsciously pick up signals from the other people, which are not just based on their words, but also on a whole array of messages coming your way.

Once I was asked how you become a deep listener and someone who was listening, and who understood the different levels of listening, said, 'You can't choose to do this, it is given to you'. I agree with this. The more you listen, the more you pick up from the other person. Whereas becoming an active listener is simply a matter of deciding to do this, becoming a deep listener just happens when we become skilled at active listening.

My most memorable example of deep listening was when I was coaching a long-term client. We would shortly be finishing our work together and he had gained so much from the coaching relationship that I suggested that he find himself a mentor. As we were talking about who might be a suitable sounding board for this very bright guy, I became aware that two parallel conversations were talking place. One was about finding the mentor and who might be suitable. The other involved him complaining vociferously about a senior manager he was working with. When I realised this was happening, I wondered if there was a link between the two conversations. I told him I was going to make a suggestion he was not going to like and then proposed that he asked the senior manager to become his mentor. He went white and then green. Then he sat back and considered the idea and decided that he would ask her. This led to a highly productive and mutually beneficial relationship that lasted a number of years. I am convinced that he was suggesting this during our conversation, but just had not quite worked out that this is what he was doing.

Now when listening to clients and friends, I listen for what people are saying but also what they are not saying. It is amazing how often this dual processing reveals some interesting insights that you would not previously have considered. I have also noticed that if people say something more than once, that this is relevant. So if you hear repetitive, almost passing, comments from someone who is not by nature repetitive, stop and think what they might be trying to tell you.

In my experience there is also a level of listening below deep listening, which engages our subconscious. Years ago I managed a careers centre for over 500 people whose jobs were being transferred to the north of the country. Since I met with so many clients and was able to keep in contact with a lot of them, over a period of months I began to realise that I was able to tell who was likely to get a job quickly simply by the way they walked in the door. There was something in their manner which suggested optimism and confidence. Of course, there might be a degree of self-fulfilling prophesy about this experience, but it taught me that even without talking, we are communicating. Other people are subconsciously reading our messages all the time, and some people can get incredibly skilled at reading people at this level.

Active and deep listening is extremely tiring and it is difficult to do this for more than a couple of hours at a time. If your work involves a lot of listening, ensure that you build in breaks to refresh yourself regularly.

The second aspects of the power of chats, comes in the form of effective questioning.

How to become a better questioner

Most people want to talk about themselves and for someone to take the trouble to listen to them. Questioning is the bridge between you and the other person. It is the way we get into someone else's world.

This should be a very simple and rewarding experience, but I have a feeling that the reason it is not done more often is not that we do not have the skill. I think it is more likely that people do not have the time or the interest to find out about another person. If you want to influence people, you must get over this barrier. People do things for people they like, and they like people who give them time and show interest in them and their lives. I once asked a woman who was incredibly popular how she achieved that. She said, 'You just keep asking them questions about themselves, and if you are lucky they will ask you something back'.

So do not expect reciprocity, just try to ask people questions until you find a point of common interest. You might feel that this is prying (and it is certainly a matter of style), but it might take them a few questions to believe that you are actually interested in them. Equally, know when to back off, if it is clear that they do not want to enter into a conversation with you.

In a coaching situation it is slightly different. Asking questions is not so difficult when you have a contractual role to facilitate change in them. Even here, I have found that you may have to repeat a question or ask it in a different way before people genuinely believe that you want to know the answer.

In our culture today, even the question 'How are you?' when you meet someone is really only a polite greeting meant to elicit the routine response 'Fine'. This is still true even if you have just split up with your partner or had some difficult news. If you go off script and actually tell someone how you feel, it is as though you have broken some unwritten formal code. So when someone asks us about ourselves, or even smiles at us, sadly we are often taken aback or suspicious of their motives.

When asking questions, whether in a business or social situation, be clear about your intentions. People pick up on intentions. If you just want to get to know them a little more or want to help them understand themselves better through answering your questions, they will appreciate that. If you want to be nosey or use questions to judge them, they will also know that.

Sometimes you can ask someone a question and they will say, 'I don't know'. This can come as a surprise when you would imagine that they would have some views on the subject. It can also be frustrating when one question is followed by another 'I don't know' answer. A technique I have borrowed from Neuro-Linguistic Programming (NLP) with some surprising outcomes is to simply say, 'And if you did know, what would you say?'. Given this fairly odd trigger question, it is interesting how many people take an intake of breath and say, 'Oh well, if I did know, I would say this …'. Somehow this very simple question seems to take the pressure off people to say what they think.

Although I have used questions in my work life very successfully for many years, I always backed off using it in my social life for fear that I was being intrusive. As a result, I could come across as rather reserved when you first met me. I then had a 'light bulb' moment and started to use the questioning skills I had developed while working with clients when meeting people socially. The effect was remarkable. After establishing rapport and engaging in some social conversation, I found that I could ask people increasingly deep and sometimes personal questions. As I did this, I found that instead of making people feel uneasy, it made them feel more comfortable. I then asked someone why he was prepared to answer some pretty personal questions about himself, and he said, 'Because I like attention'.

Throughout this book I have been attempting not just to encourage you to take certain actions, but also to explain how to do it. When it comes to questioning, it is harder to give you a definitive approach, since it is such a matter of style and chemistry for both parties. Part of me says just try some well-intentioned 'poking about'; the other part of me says do not try this unless you can find some genuine interest in the person, the answers they are likely to give or what they are saying.

The flip side of getting people to talk about what they want to talk about is using probing questions to gain specific information. Probing questions are particularly useful to find out what is happening with a person, team, organisation or family, below the surface. I once worked with someone who was incredibly good at creating change in her organisation, particularly in relation to reducing budgets and changing departmental spending behaviour. When I asked her how she achieved this, it was clear that she was highly skilled at asking probing questions. Whereas her colleagues might read the 'riot act' to budget holders, she asked them probing questions, which enabled her to examine their spending habits and what they could change.

If you are on the receiving end of this type of question, it may make you feel uncomfortable, but it will make you very aware of issues that you may not have been aware of or that you preferred to overlook. When faced with a major need to get departments to control their budgets and cut costs, I advised her to pass on this valuable skill to other members of her team.

Probing questions involve 'drilling down' the issue to get more information. A very common way of doing this is to take the answer you are given to a question and then to ask a series of 'why?' or 'how?' questions to gain more information.

It is remarkable how much additional information can be gained in this way, but you must do it with a degree of subtlety to avoid sounding like an interrogator or a robot. It is a very useful tool to raise self-awareness and to highlight patterns, if done in a sensitive and persistent manner.

Questions are very powerful. By showing interest in another person, you bestow a huge gift on them. You also need to remember that once people have opened up to you, you have a duty of trust and confidentiality. People's ideas and inner thoughts are precious to them and they should be precious to you. If you have acquired the ability to get people to talk about themselves, do not abuse this trust by sharing what they would prefer you not to disclose with others who may be interested to hear it.

Learn to love the void

I want to say something about the power of the void. The void is an empty space. Lots of people do not like an empty space and will rush to fill it. I want to encourage you to learn to love the void.

I first noticed the power of the void many years ago, when I was on a diving holiday, staying on a boat with a group of people. I had just become aware that I had a tendency to criticise people when speaking to them. Because it was a habitual pattern, I simply did not realise that there was a link between my behaviour and people feeling uneasy in my company and moving away.

The moment I made this connection, I stopped being critical. What followed was very unpleasant. I just did not know what to say instead of my critical comments. It was as though a void had opened up. It would have been very easy to go back to the comments that I was comfortable with. Instead, I lived with the void – the horrible feeling that I had nothing to say. After a few days, new thoughts and ideas started to come into the void. I began to adopt some healthier behaviours and started to notice people becoming more relaxed around me. Living with the void had been instrumental in helping me move from one place to another, as gradually unhelpful patterns were replaced by much more productive ones.

The void is also a concept that I use in coaching situations and it can be incredibly helpful in listening and questioning. When I am questioning, I take the time to create the space for people to talk and do not interrupt the silence. Most people feel uncomfortable with spaces and pauses and they tend to rush in to fill them.

When working with a client (a director of finance) who was extremely stressed and had incredibly high standards for herself and the team, I made the observation that if she never allowed a void to appear, she would always be picking up most of the work. I encouraged her to learn to live with the void. She looked shocked, and even getting her to think about this had clearly moved her out of her comfort zone. Her level of reaction convinced me that this is what she needed to do. This would be incredibly challenging for her, but until she allowed the void to appear, she would never make any headway on her tendency to take on more of her share of the work. Once she allowed the void to appear, other people began to pick up the work. This is what she wrote about her experience of managing the void:

> 'Entering into a new role it's difficult to leave the old one behind. It can be unbearable to watch someone else do 'your job' – but not do it as well as you. It takes standing back to realise (and accept) it's not about doing the job as well as me – just accepting that it's different. Learning to 'let go' is rather like a grieving process. It was only when my inclination and habit to 'wade in' to situations was described as 'entering the void' that I then learnt to 'keep my distance' and wait to give help only when it is sought. Let others make their own mistakes.

Skilled negotiators also understand the power of the void by creating a space or pause in the discussions. Since many people are uncomfortable with silence or pausing, negotiators realise that the person who is most uncomfortable with the silence is the one who is likely to make the next move. This gives the more relaxed negotiator the opportunity to respond to their comments or proposals.

It takes practice

Moving out of your comfort zone can, by definition, be very uncomfortable, but it is only when you are prepared to try new behaviours – even when the new behaviour is doing nothing – that you can start to form new habits. The more you step out of your comfort zone, the more your comfort zone will increase and include a bigger range of skills and possibilities.

You now have some new insights into building rapport, different types of communication style, the hierarchy of language, establishing your credibility, listening and questioning, and managing the void. If you integrate all of these skills into a systematic approach using the cycle of influence, you should be ready to have some powerful and influential conversations.

Although it can sound as though there is a lot to remember, think back to when you first learnt to drive a car, maybe master a sport, or play a musical instrument – you probably felt the same way. First of all, you had to learn the basic skills and then apply your knowledge continuously until you achieved an improved performance. When you first started, it might all have seemed very challenging and chaotic. What probably kept you going was your desire to achieve the end result. Learning to influence does take time and practice and you will not get it right first time.

When you begin to influence, plan your interactions with people. Let go of your previous assumptions about yourself and others, and start to focus on each success. Gradually you will find that each time you approach a situation, your outcomes will get better and better.

When I tell people that I had to learn these skills myself, they often say something like, 'Oh, but you do them so naturally'. My usual reply is that it has taken me a lot of work and effort to become a 'natural'. If you learn these skills, you will come across to other people as more confident and friendly. You will soon be able to walk into any situation, knowing that you will come across as relaxed and comfortable. In the process you will start to put other people at their ease too. Once you start to achieve this, you will start to have conversations that lead to outcomes you did not previously believe possible.

I have covered a lot of ground in this section on influencing since they are core skills that you will build on as you move up the continuum of interpersonal skills. Take your time to integrate the skills and get comfortable them.

Pamela was my coach for a whole year as part of a management programme. We met on a monthly basis and I really looked forward to our sessions.

I have to say that I was not buying into the whole concept during the first session, interpreting influencing as manipulating and against my quite well defined and strong principles.

This changed quickly as Pamela teaches you to understand the social and cultural background of the person you are working with and I adapted her techniques to get the results.

This means that the method she has developed is based on core principles that can be adapted efficiently in a wide range of situations.

I am not by training or profession a "manager". (I am a Consultant Anaesthetist.) However I came to realise that a lot of what I do requires some managerial skills.

Pamela also made me realise that I already possessed some of the skills needed but was not necessarily using them to their full potential.

Using her techniques I came to know myself better and started enjoying my managerial role.

Looking back on our sessions, what remains with me is that there was almost a psychological analysis of a situation which was translated into a systematic approach and this, I found, was a very powerful learning tool.

I have now known Pamela for many years and I am using what she taught me all the time but most of the time without realising it. This is what makes the content of her book important. This is not a technique but an analysis of situations and personalities which gives an understanding of how to unlock the potentials of one self and others.

As you get increasingly more skilled at any activity, you want to do more of it and go on to the next level. Human interaction in this way is no different from any other discipline. When people become excellent influencers, they tend to put their head above the parapet and say, 'OK, what's next?'.

The next set of skills up the continuum of interpersonal skills is learning the art of negotiation.

Reactionnaire

What are your beliefs around becoming an effective influencer?

What are your thoughts on the influencing skills that I have covered in this chapter?

What feelings did you experience as you read the information on influencing that was covered in this chapter?

What ideas 'popped into your head' as you read through the infliuencing skills?

What actions are you going to take as a result of reading the section on Influencing?

Top Tips to become more influential: see
page 182.

Chapter 7
Negotiation

The Continuum of Interpersonal Skills – Negotiation

The significant difference between influencing and negotiation is that when you influence someone, they are happy to do something for you. They do this either because you have persuaded them that it is worthwhile or because they spontaneously want to assist you. In negotiation, it is a trade-off – in return for something they do, they will want something back from you.

In exchange for some effort, time, money or resources on your part, the other party wants to gain some benefit in terms of effort, time, money or resources on their part. In other words, both of you have agendas. Both of you want to get your needs met and to maximise what you get out of the agreement. When done well, negotiation can be upbeat, humorous and enjoyable. When done badly, it can be frustrating, fruitless and damaging to both parties and the organisations they represent.

People who are assertive and influential make the best negotiators, since they understand themselves and how other people operate. Negotiators without these skills tend to take an 'I positive, you negative' stance with others, and try to force their opponents into agreement. Alternatively, they can adopt an 'I negative, you positive' stance and walk away from negotiations on unfavourable terms.

For many years, at the end of a negotiation programme, I asked people to negotiate a low-risk scenario. What always fascinated me during this exercise was how, given exactly the same facts, the participants would agree on, or in some cases not agree on, radically different outcomes. Some people did not stand their ground and were not clear about what they wanted to achieve. Others approached it aggressively and hammered their opponents into submission. These tendencies were reflected in the final result. The pairs who achieved the best outcomes and seemed to enjoy themselves in the process understood the principles of negotiation: that it is a gradual process of revealing your agenda and uncovering their agenda to identify the overlap between 'wants' and to establish where a deal can be done. They tended to build rapport with their partners, adopt a friendly and relaxed style and know where they were in the negotiation process at any given point.

In other words, successful negotiation is as much about having a positive outlook, using basic interpersonal skills, treating the other party with respect, dealing with deflections, two-way communication and not losing sight of the goal, as it is about learning technical moves and tactics.

You cannot be an effective negotiator if you are not assertive and if you have a tendency to be passive. If you show your hand too early, buckle under pressure, get the timing wrong or have a resistance to being in a game, you will not be able to achieve successful outcomes. If you do not have these skills and you do not believe you can achieve a good outcome, you are likely to negotiate with yourself before you begin the negotiation with the other party.

The impact of beliefs on negotiations

Before I go on to outline the skills of negotiation, I want to say something about the role of beliefs.

Some early readers of this book, many with very high-level interpersonal skills, told me that they have a mental block when it comes to negotiating, particularly when negotiating on their own behalf. One client told me that his negative beliefs in relation to being an effective negotiator were as follows.

- I just feel I am not good at it.
- I don't prepare enough.
- My judgement on when to cut a deal is not great.
- I should share less information.

If you want to be a successful negotiator, you must get over any negative thinking. When reading this chapter, if you feel some resistance to using the skills and working within the structure suggested, go back to the negative belief cycle explained in Chapter 3 and explore why you feel this way. Once you have identified which of your negative beliefs might be hampering you, explore their effect and select some more positive beliefs to open up the possibility that you can be an effective negotiator.

I once worked with a group who commissioned services from another group in the public sector. The commissioners strongly believed that since they were essentially working for the same organisation, they should just say what they wanted to buy and at what cost and that should be the end of it. They were then very surprised when the provider organisation, which had considerably more expertise in this arena, started negotiating with them in terms of both cost and quantity. As a result, their entire planning process was 'thrown into disarray' because they did not understand how negotiation works.

The negotiation game

Negotiation is like playing chess: you move one piece and, in response, the other party makes a counter-move. You then look at the board to reconsider your tactics before making the next move. It can be a game that is highly enjoyable and stimulating to both players. In contrast, if you are discussing international agreements, each move can be pivotal, can be potentially risky and can impact on long-term security or financial stability.

Whatever form it takes, negotiation is a fascinating, complex interplay between the two key parties, combining high-level interpersonal skills, experience, positive belief systems, support networks and confidence. Excellent negotiators are secure in themselves, can build rapport, establish their credibility and are prepared to ask for what they want.

As we move up the continuum of interpersonal skills, you will notice that the skills you are accumulating are becoming much more subtle and sophisticated. In terms of the continuum, the main skill that is added at the level of negotiation is respect for boundaries – your own and the other party's. Despite the requirement to sound vague you have to be clear about what your requirements are and what you are seeking from the other party. You have to ensure that you do not get sidetracked or drawn into fruitless discussion; be clear about where you are in the negotiation at any point in the process.

My advice is to take your time to prepare and learn the stages of negotiation. Do not rush the process, be clear about what stage you are in at any given moment, and when you get confused (and you **will** get confused) take time out to review your thoughts and decide on your next tactical move.

The rules of negotiation

Before you can begin to play the negotiation game, you have to understand the rules. These are as follows.

- Go for a 'win-win' outcome, which suits both parties.
- Work out what you want to achieve and what it is worth to you.
- Do not 'lay all your cards on the table'. If you do, you will have nowhere to go, should your offer be rejected.
- Do not give up anything without getting something in return.
- Do not make another offer before they have responded to your original offer.
- Use questioning techniques to find out what their agendas are.
- Keep things multifactorial and trade one factor for another factor.
- Nothing is settled until everything is settled.
- Avoid criticising the other party – it delays achieving a successful outcome.
- Respond to attempts to deflect you from your aim through flattery or criticism by using assertiveness techniques.
- Focus on outcomes, not on the behaviour or personality of the other party.
- Use the power of pausing to allow what you have said to 'settle in the air' and to be considered by the other party.
- Reveal some of your agendas in order to learn some of their agendas.
- Be prepared to walk away from the negotiation, if there is no overlap in your agendas or if you cannot achieve a mutually beneficial agreement.

The theory of negotiation

There are numerous excellent books on negotiation and nearly all of them promote a four-, five-, six-, seven- or even eight-stage model.

Gavin Kennedy, in his book *Perfect Negotiation*[5], recommends a four-stage model – prepare, debate, propose, bargain – which is straightforward and works extremely well.

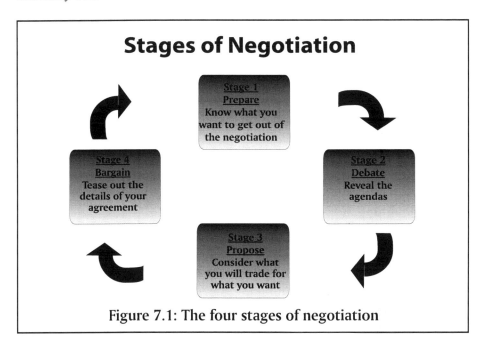

Figure 7.1: The four stages of negotiation

Source: Adapted from Kennedy, 2003.

The four stages of negotiation are:

- **Stage 1: Prepare** – know what you want to get out of the negotiation
- **Stage 2: Debate** – reveal the agendas
- **Stage 3: Propose** – consider what you could trade or give up in return for what you want
- **Stage 4: Bargain** – tease out the details of your agreement.

In negotiation always aim to be at one of these stages and to know which stage you are at. If you find the process going out of control, it is probably because you have got ahead of yourself or made a few too many assumptions about what the other

5   Random House Business 2003

party wants or needs. If this happens, backtrack to the stage where you might have lost the plot, clarify where you are and start again from there.

So let's take these stages one at a time.

Stage 1: Prepare – know what you want to get out of the negotiation

As we have seen in the chapters on assertiveness (Chapter 5) and influencing (Chapter 6), a great deal of the success you will have in your interactions with others is down to how much planning and preparation you put in beforehand. When negotiating, preparation is even more important. The main concern involves working out your ideal position and reading the total picture to see if you can work out the other party's ideal position. The deal you strike in any negotiation happens in the space where an overlap exists between the two agendas. The crucial skill in negotiating is to identify if this overlap exists and predict where the point of agreement might be. If there is no overlap, no deal is possible, and trying to continue to negotiate where there is no overlap will just irritate both parties.

Do your research to find out what is a possible outcome and what is a probable outcome. Decide what you want to achieve and write it down. Create a list of wants. Some of these wants will be essential (high value), some will be desirable (medium value) and some will just be there because they would be nice to have and can be used as bargaining tools (low value).

Quantify your wants in terms of money, time, resources, quantity, quality, or adherence to personal (and possibly illogical) preferences or principles. Then assess what these factors mean to you.

When preparing your wants list, consider the following questions.

- What is this negotiation worth to you?
- What factors should be on your wants list?
- Where can you obtain all the facts you need?
- Who else do you need to talk to?
- What calculations do you need to make in actual numbers and percentages?
- What are your entry and exit points?
- What outcomes have others achieved in a similar situation?

Table 7.1 is a sample negotiation preparation grid, which will help you to draw up your list of wants.

Table 7.1: Sample negotiation preparation grid

Negotiation issues	Wants	Relative Importance	Range entry point	Range exit point

Have a number of factors on your preparation grid (even some which are not particularly important to you) in order to trade what you do not really want or need for what you really do want or need.

Entry points indicate your ideal scenario and are where you will start in the negotiation process. These should be realistic, credible and defensible and should avoid antagonising the other party. Exit points indicate the least you are prepared to accept. This is your 'walking away' position and will depend on how many alternative options you have.

In the preparation stage, aim to create a clear picture of your wants and their relative importance.

Table 7.2 is a completed negotiation preparation grid, using the example of a house purchase.

Table 7.2: Example of a completed negotiation preparation grid

Negotiation issues	Wants	Relative importance	Range entry point	Range exit point
Value of mortgage	Not more than £120K	Very high	£80K	£120k
Likes a bargain	Essential to get a deal	Very high	Make an opportunistic offer	Make a realistic offer based on current knowledge

Negotiation issues	Wants	Relative importance	Range entry point	Range exit point
Is ready to move straight away	To move quickly	Medium	Complete in two weeks, as have mortgage no need to give notice	Usual time required to do conveyancing
Additional car parking space	Get another space in car park	Very low	Do not want to pay any more for this	Would not walk away if did not get it
To keep carpets, curtains and fittings	Keep everything currently in the property	Very high. Cannot afford the property if items are not included or very cheap	To pay nothing	To pay no more than £6k
To have show-house accessories	Show off property to best effect, would love to keep them if possible	Very low	Nothing	Monetary value zero – would be nice to have
All prepared positions may change as the negotiation unfolds.				

When planning your negotiation strategy, have as many wants as you can generate. Some will be an important requirement for you and some a low requirement, which you can concede easily. Realise that some factors that may have a high significance to you, may have a low value to the other party. Equally, some factors which may be insignificant to you, may have a high value for them.

In the house-buying scenario in Table 7.2, two representatives of the developers had suggested that they would accept an offer. Both of them indicated a figure, which was higher than the buyer wanted to pay, although it was clear that they were very keen to sell. In this example, a high 'want' for the developer was to complete the deal by the end of the financial year. Although an early completion date had a medium value for the buyer, by understanding the wants of the developer and holding their boundaries, the purchaser was able to get the deal they wanted, with the carpets, fittings and show-house accessories included, providing they completed within three-and-a-half weeks to meet the end of the financial year. The awareness of the other party's high-priority wants enabled an excellent bargain to be made.

While I am aware that this may not be the most sophisticated example of negotiation you might come across, it does give you some idea of the preparation process that needs to be done before you start negotiating. In many ways it is better to start small to understand the process and gain some experience, rather than getting into high-level, complicated negotiations, which may become messy and out of control.

Once you have completed your 'wants' list, prepare for the debate stage.

Stage 2: Debate – Reveal the agendas

The multifactorial nature of negotiating is part of the 'game' and allows you to gradually reveal your agenda, while gradually uncovering the other party's agenda.

The debate stage is all about using questioning and listening skills. Look for clues and signals. Be prepared to give clues and signals yourself. Use vague language to indicate your wants, for example 'It would be nice if you could do something about the quantity of the order'. Ask loose, vague questions to indicate your curiosity about their 'wants' list, for example 'I was wondering if you ever do discounts?'.

As much as anything this is about energy. Look for signs that they want to do a deal, how much effort they are putting into it and how many clues they are giving you that a deal may be possible. When they say 'I am sure we can come to a mutually acceptable agreement', you know they are keen.

If a 'want' is not on the negotiating table now, it will not get included in the bargaining stage or the final outcome. Asking for additional 'wants' later in the process irritates the other party and sets the negotiation back to the previous stage. That is if you are lucky. If you are unlucky, they may just walk away, thinking that just when they get close to a deal, you will move the goalposts and make a deal impossible. Negotiating is about having clear boundaries and using high-level interpersonal skills to gradually funnel the decisions to an end point where both of you agree with the outcome.

Most of the time spent negotiating should be at the debate stage. Do not go on to the next stage before you are confident that you have gathered all the details you need from the other party and revealed a significant number of your wants to them. When you have all the information about the other party that you can obtain, and have revealed as much about your position as you can, ideally you should take a break to reflect on what you have discovered. Talk to colleagues, do more research and plan your next move. In fact, this opportunity to reflect is so important that it might be worth considering if you can get the other party to agree to this at the beginning and build it into the agenda.

Thinking time and pausing is usually extremely beneficial to both parties. If you cannot build it into the process, take a comfort break or become an 'honorary' smoker – go outside for a few minutes to clear your thoughts. As you move away from the situation, a lot of factors will fall into place and your ideas will become more focused.

The key question to ask at the debate stage is: 'Is there a deal to be done here?'. The answer to this is not always about the numbers; sometimes it is about willingness and energy. I once entered into a negotiation where the numbers were far apart. However, it was clear from the other party's energy and willingness to engage that there was a deal to be done there – I just had to be more probing as to why they were still at the negotiating table.

The following checklist will help you to prepare for the meeting, set the scene and ensure that your conversation stays focused during your discussions.

Table 7.3: The debate stage checklist

Elements	Comments
Build rapport	Consider their interests, communication style and where they are in the organisation or hierarchy.
Set and agree the agenda	What is the agenda for the meeting? How will you describe the process, so that both parties agree to follow the 'debate, propose and bargain' structure?
Describe what you are seeking	Decide what language you will use to allude to your agenda without directly telling them your prepared positions. Useful phrases are: 'I would like...'; 'I am willing to be constructive'; 'My intention is...' You want to set a scene, not give away the total picture.
Listen and question	Negotiation is an art, not a science. It is about working out your position and listening for clues that give away the other party's position. So aim to do as much listening as talking. 80% of negotiation should be at the debate stage, so take your time to ask questions, which will elicit what may be on the other party's prepared list. Open questions unlock doors. The more you can get them to talk, the better. The more relaxed they are, the more likely they are to share their agenda. Ask vague but deceptively deep questions, for example 'I was wondering what you had in mind?' or 'are you able to do anything better than that?' then stay silent and wait for them to answer.

Elements	Comments
Identify available incentives or threats to facilitate movement	Think about how you could 'dangle' some incentives they might like, but which cost you virtually nothing. Consider how you might allude to any consequences that might happen if they do not come to an agreement with you, e.g. 'Do you realise that none of the money will be released until we have agreed all parts of the deal?'.
Look for signals	People give out signals all the time. If they are enthusiastic, they will be animated. If they are disinterested, they will be flat. Look for energy. Press a few buttons and see what moves you closer or further away from your goal. If people say something more than once, it is important to them – even if they may not be aware of this themselves.
Respond to signals	If they make a suggestion you do not like, try not to criticise or (worse still) laugh. Instead, make a vague statement to indicate that this is not really what you had in mind, e.g. 'Our usual approach is ...'; 'It would be extremely difficult'.
Respond to deflections	It is possible during the negotiation, particularly if things are not going as hoped, that the other party may flatter or criticise you in order to sidetrack the discussions. Recognise the behaviour and use the assertiveness techniques discussed in Chapter 5 to respond to deflections.
Read the energy put into the discussion by the other party	Are they showing signs of wanting to achieve a bargain, even if there does not appear to be an overlap in your wants? If so, continue to use probing questions to find out why they are still engaging in the negotiation process.
Take a break	Take breaks if you need to reflect on your position. The best negotiators often appear to have weak bladders.

Based on what you have learnt in the debate stage, you should now be ready to enter Stage 3 – Propose. Here you start making proposals and hearing proposals from them that will form the basis for agreement.

Stage 3: Propose – consider what you could trade or give up in return for what you want

Again, your language should be vague. Offers should be conditional and suggest that you will do something if they do something in return. The sentence structure of an offer is: 'If you do that for me, I will do this you'. Consider all the factors in the negotiation simultaneously and keep all of them on the negotiating table. Do not negotiate items on your wants list individually – keep them all dependent on each other and nothing should be settled until everything is settled.

Keep track of what you are proposing and make a note of their response. Make vague statements to express your interests, for example, 'I might be able to do this, if you would consider doing that'.

Do not aggravate the other party by making your opening offers unrealistic. If they do not seem keen or excited, slow down, back off and reconsider your position. If they are too eager to accept your first offer, you have probably pitched it far too generously. To avoid this, make sure that your first offer is realistic but on the cautious side.

If they do not like your proposals, or you do not like their proposals, suggest a counter-offer. Keep all factors linked, until you have an idea where the overlaps in your wants and needs may be and have identified the middle ground where a deal can be done. Remember that some factors that might be very important to you, might be insignificant to them. These can be given to you at virtually no additional cost or effort. For example, if you are planning a conference, it might be very easy for a conference centre to provide an additional space for you to put up marketing information and where your guests can relax and hold discussions. This could be a very valuable asset for you and may cost the conference centre virtually nothing to give you this benefit as a concession as part of the negotiation process.

If you can, plan in another interval before the next stage.

Having tested the boundaries and parameters for possible agreements, you should now be ready for the final stage: the bargain.

Stage 4: Bargain – tease out the details of your agreement

When negotiating the bargaining stage, the language is no longer vague. It is based on hard facts, figures, dates, targets, incentives and deadlines. Write down the bargain and ensure that you agree and have a shared perception about the outcome reached. If both parties understand the negotiation process and have equal skill and self-confidence, it should be a 'win-win' outcome.

That is the theory. In reality, negotiation is a lot more disjointed. It can get very personal and can be hijacked by the vested interests of third parties. It can also become protracted, due to illogical and often hidden agendas, and can go on for much longer than is truly necessary. Like a game of chess, it is a fascinating and complex interplay between the two main protagonists.

Negotiation in practice

I consider myself a skilled negotiator and just cannot stop myself doing it. I will negotiate anything given the opportunity, but it has not always been that way. Although I trained people in negotiating skills, I did not quite internalise the process until I had to take on a significant negotiation myself. The factors involved were complex and it affected me on an emotional level. At the same time I was lucky to have a lawyer, who was an expert negotiator, assisting me to navigate through the process.

These are the lessons I have learnt from my own experiences of negotiation.

- Everything has a value – you just need to work out what it is worth.
- Stick to the facts – avoid getting sidetracked.
- If you are bullied, calmly suggest that the behaviour is unacceptable and outline any sanctions that can be applied.
- Look for buying signals and pay attention to any interests revealed by the other party.
- Discuss the issues with someone you respect, who is not emotionally involved.
- If you have made a proposal, sit and wait for a response – do not fill the gap with another proposal.
- Do not give up any benefits without concessions in return.
- A deal is not done until it is final and the contract is signed.
- Right at the end, when you seem to be getting on well, do not offer favourable last-minute concessions.

I make deals on virtually anything, from industrial contracts to computer software and artwork, saving thousands of pounds each year in the process. I enjoy negotiating and want to share a very practical negotiation experience with you because it demonstrates very well the game-playing element involved in achieving a win-win outcome.

My car needed some expensive repairs and was coming up for its yearly inspection, so I decided to buy a new one rather than get it repaired. Due to the 'credit crunch', car dealers were going through a very bad time. There were very few buyers and a lot of sellers. Although I knew what car I wanted and the listed price, none of the dealerships I approached seemed very interested in making a sale (preparation).

Finally I found a salesman who clearly loved to negotiate. During the debate stage he correctly identified that I wanted to take delivery of the car immediately, even though I was trying not to look keen. He worked out that I liked the leather steering wheel (a minor factor, but of high importance to me). He also noticed that the length of the car was significant in my decision, because when parking I like to nip into small spaces. Unlike another salesmen I had spoken to, he took my interest seriously. He arranged for the car I wanted to brought from the depot in under an hour so I could see it, while making a point of saying that this put me under no obligation to buy. During my test drive, I received messages from dealers regarding appointments to see other cars, and I mentioned this to him in passing when we were back at the showroom.

He encouraged me to tell him what figure I had in mind and he told me the book price for the car I wanted to buy. I decided to pitch my entry-level offer low to judge his reaction, and I stayed in that region for a while. A couple of times during our 'little chat' he sucked in his teeth and said, 'That's impossible'. He discussed the situation with his manager and came back and shook his head. The manager joined us and confirmed that it was indeed impossible to sell me a car at that price and both of them sat there, pessimistically and sympathetically shaking their heads.

Reluctantly, although I was clearly a willing buyer and he was clearly a very willing seller, there appeared to be no deal to be done that day, since there was no overlap in our wants. I felt frustrated, but did not feel able to move on my 'exit point' position. I left the showroom without leaving my details and sat in my car. I did not leave the car park. Instead, in full view of the salesman, I rang a colleague who had offered to discuss tactics with me. He suggested that I went back into the showroom, restated my interest in buying the car and invited the salesman to give me a call if he changed his mind.

The salesman seeing me approach again, clearly thinking I was coming back to buy the car, became animated. Instead I simply restated my intention to buy, if he reconsidered his position. Straightaway he knocked another few hundred off the price of the car. This was starting to look like quite a good deal, although it still was not achieving what I wanted and still did not match what I thought the car was 'worth' to me. I acted unimpressed, restated the figure I wanted to pay for it, reconfirmed my interest should he change his mind and left (this demonstrates the use of pause).

That night he rang me to propose a deal, which was only £100 off my ideal price, provided I could produce the service history for my current car (a classic 'If you do this, I will do that' proposal). I am pretty sure that I could have reduced the price further, but I decided that the salesman had done an excellent job. He had been polite, respectful, entertaining and proactive, and he wanted the business. I did not want to overplay my hand for such a small amount. I seized the deal, not because it was overgenerous, but because it was pitched at exactly the right level.

Effective negotiation is the meeting of the minds of two equals. If you have developed all the earlier skills and you follow the structure for negotiation I have outlined above, you will not only achieve successful outcomes, but you (and the other party) will also enjoy the process. Excellent negotiators can spot other excellent negotiators and enjoy the intellectual tussle that a good bargain can create.

If you can combine these skills with the other skills that you have already acquired as you move up the continuum of interpersonal skills, you will find yourself achieving outcomes that you never thought possible and will save yourself a lot of time, money and frustration in the process.

Using negotiation skills responsibly

As I mentioned in Chapter 4, the skills of the exceptional influencer and negotiator are also the skills of an arch-manipulator. What makes the difference between the two stances is the intention. If you intend not only to do well for yourself, but also to enhance the community in which you operate, people will pick this up, work with you and want to be around you. If you use the skills to manipulate people, they will resent it. If you are manipulating people, it might take a while for them to work out what you are doing, particularly if you become very skilled at the strategies I have described. But in the end, they will work it out and will try to avoid engaging with you.

For many of my clients, having these skills can appear to 'go to their heads', albeit temporarily, and I have to remind them to use their skills responsibly. I have noticed a few times that when clients bask in the sense of what they can do, they consider taking on challenges that might push the boundaries between influencing and trying to take too much control over events. I think that is a very human thing to do and we all do it sometimes. Reviewing your behaviour in the context of your intentions can be a useful filter to help you decide whether you are flexing your skills, or fighting that battle, just because you can.

Choosing not to use your skills when you know you can, but perhaps you should not, takes a great deal of restraint. Using these skills responsibly is a challenge, and you need to be aware of the temptation you might have to use them to advance your own ends to the detriment of others.

There is another facet to learning high-level interpersonal skills that you might want to consider. One of my very skilled clients working at board level used a term 'on the side of the angels' when talking about one of his colleagues. This comment surprised me, particularly since he is working in a financial environment and that is not the usual language of an accountant. When I thought about it afterwards, this phrase perfectly sums up the position of using your people skills with a good intention. You just begin to get a sense of who you can trust and work with and who might be a bit more difficult to deal with.

I have observed that even supreme tacticians who have acquired the systematic and incremental skills outlined in this book, despite the obvious temptations, will then begin to use them in a slightly different way. They know they can 'beat' anyone who might challenge them, yet they choose not to.

My interpretation of this behaviour takes us back to where we started. Always winning is not an assertive stance nor even an enjoyable one, since it is in effect an 'I positive, you negative' position. So to maintain the delicate 'I positive, you positive' balance, people operating at this level start to become more conciliatory to the other party. Instead of setting out to win, they begin to share their knowledge with others, sometimes even up-skilling the people or groups who might be traditionally regarded as their opponents.

At this level, people begin to get a reputation for remaining calm under pressure, having clear boundaries, and using process skills to work towards agreements. They are respected by a wide range of people for their fairness and consistency. Due to these skills and qualities, when disputes or conflicts arise, people naturally turn to them to see if they can assist the aggrieved parties to come to a resolution.

Once you have integrated the skills of negotiation into you 'tool box' of interpersonal skills the next level up the continuum of interpersonal skills is conciliation.

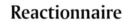

Reactionnaire

What are your beliefs around your ability to negotiate successfully?

What are your thoughts on the negotiation skills that I have covered in this chapter?

What feelings did you experience as you read the information on negotiation that was covered in this chapter?

What ideas 'popped into your head' as you read through the negotiation skills?

What actions are you going to take as a result of reading the section on negotiation?

Top Tips to become an effective
negotiator: see page 183.

127

Chapter 8
Conciliation

The Continuum of Interpersonal Skills – Conciliation

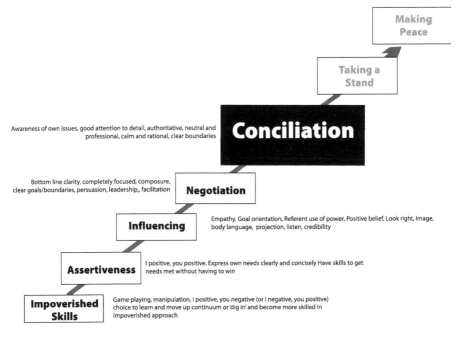

Having witnessed this movement up the continuum of interpersonal skills towards conciliation with a number of my regular board-level coaching clients, I believe that the pattern is common enough to be considered a tendency. People progress naturally through the stages, as they build on the skills they have achieved at the previous level.

Natural Conciliation Skills – a Story

The most colourful story I have come across in relation to the skills of conciliation is when Dahir Kadiye, a former taxi driver from Leytonstone, East London stepped in to conciliate with Somali pirates. He took it upon himself to broker the release of Paul and Rachel Chandler who were captured while sailing off the Seychelles coast in October 2009. In this instance he was conciliating between the pirates and the Somali community who felt very aggrieved by the kidnapping. When talking about his successful mission in November 2010 Mr Kadiye was remarkably understated and said he got involved in the hostage negotiation after his children told him they felt ashamed to be Somalis after seeing the story on television.

Later one of his relatives almost casually commented on his achievements by suggesting that Mr Kadiye was always invited in to handle the disputes, which broke out in the family and the community.

The Oxford Dictionary defines conciliation as 'the action of mediating between two disputing people or groups' The case of the Somali hostages demonstrates very well that you do not have to legal training to be a effective conciliator but for understandable reasons due to the high level of skill required to achieve a desirable outcome it often becomes the domain of lawyers and professional mediators or conciliators.

Since I believe that at each level on the continuum people display patterns of behaviour, I was interested to find out what those patterns were at the conciliation stage.

From my observation, people who become conciliators – whether in the playground, boardroom, court room or on the world stage – have similar characteristics. Apart from being confident and comfortable with themselves, they have the power to get their needs met through behaviour that most people would hardly notice. They are deceptively skilled and charming. They are respectful and supportive to others. Sometimes they just turn up and have a chat and then items on the agenda start to move forward towards their identified goal.

So far I have described a natural progression through the continuum of interpersonal skills and how success at one level inspires enthusiasm for the next level up. For some people this process may happen even without formally learning the skills I have outlined. In other words, an enthusiastic amateur can achieve the outcomes I have described so far. Combine positive beliefs with the relevant skills set and a readiness to change your behaviour to achieve the desired goals and you will be achieving results you did not think possible. Conciliation is different. Conciliation discussions can be emotionally sensitive, because of the very delicate nature of the issues involved. I believe that unless you have the unusual skill and confidence of someone like Dahir Kadiye conciliation skills must be actively learnt. To enhance my own skills and assist clients to develop themselves in this area, I attended a course run by Acas (Advisory, Conciliation and Arbitration Service).

Effective conciliators have all the skills that we have discussed so far in this book. They also have positive beliefs about themselves and their ability to influence others. In the process they will also have gained positive beliefs about other people and will have an insight into their motivations and intentions. In other words, successful conciliators will have a track record of success.

What is added at this level in terms of skill is the ability to keep boundaries absolutely clear and to encourage others to describe events without emotional labelling or judgement. They then work towards an agreement that both parties can accept, using a clear and transparent structure. This structure keeps the process on track during the conversations, while always working towards a constructive conclusion.

A conciliator knows that they have considerable skills, but instead of using those skills to achieve goals for themselves, they use those skills for the benefit of others. Unlike the previous interpersonal stages, which might involve some forceful discussions, during conciliation they may also be dealing with highly emotionally charged situations.

Although types of conflict can vary from major international troubles to work or family disputes, the root causes of the problem might be the same. These include:

- cultural or religious differences
- personality clashes
- varying communication styles
- incompatible beliefs
- no strategies for resolving conflicts
- a lack of respect for the circumstances of the other person.

This is compounded when the main protagonists themselves may not know why they are experiencing such intense feelings and reactions to each other and to events. Many disputes start in a relatively minor way and escalate as grievances are piled onto other grievances.

During negotiation, the issues being discussed are multifactorial. During conciliation, they are multifactorial combined with the need to deal with the emotional reactions of the parties involved. Here one word out of place can throw the whole meeting out of kilter. A conciliator needs to steer the meeting and ensure that all significant issues that have been identified have a forum during the discussion.

The role of the conciliator is twofold: to manage the conciliation process; and to manage the conciliation task. Both have to be done in a highly professional and sophisticated manner to create an environment of trust and resolution.

Managing the conciliation process

For the conciliator, the key issues in managing the conciliation process are to:

- believe that they can use their skills to enable others to resolve disputes
- maintain positive beliefs about people
- respect themselves and others
- remain calm under pressure – often disarmingly so
- use reactions and feelings to inform themselves, but not to act on them
- see the person behind the problem
- have clear personal boundaries
- maintain complete fairness and equality
- avoid defending or attacking
- not take criticism personally
- accept and respect the beliefs of others
- act with judgement
- ensure confidentiality
- empathise
- keep language neutral.

Managing the conciliation task

For the conciliator, the key issues in managing the conciliation task are to:

- build trust in themselves as a conciliator and in the conciliation process

- use a highly structured approach to explore concerns
- share the structure of the conciliation process
- create an environment of trust
- gain commitment to engage in the conciliation process
- manage expectations
- ensure that the systematic approach is followed
- ask questions and listen in order to identify key themes
- focus on facts and behaviour
- enable concerned parties to reflect on their behaviour
- avoid deviations from the task
- create summaries
- work towards solutions
- write down agreements.

The four stages of conciliation

These roles of managing the process and managing the task can be translated into a four-stage model.

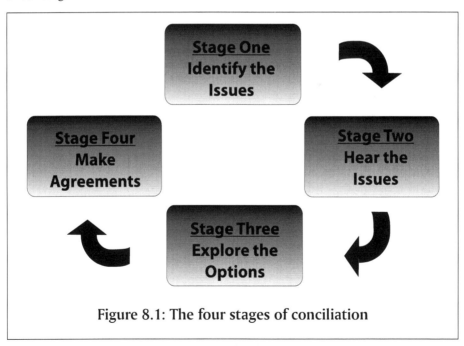

Figure 8.1: The four stages of conciliation

Source: Adapted from Acas mediation model 2007[6]

6   Mediation process stages and key tasks Acas 2007

Stage 1: Identify the issues with each individual

In this stage you need to make an arrangement to meet with both parties individually at a suitable time and place to explore the issues.

It is likely that at least one of them (maybe both) will be emotional. Your task as conciliator is to listen to their concerns, which might be all over the place and interspersed with anger or hurt. From these often jumbled events and feelings you need to tease out the key issues

When you first meet each person on their own, start to develop a relationship of trust. Do this by sharing something about yourself, which establishes your credibility to manage the task. Explain the conciliation process and your role within it. Emphasise that you will be guiding the process, acting as an impartial witness and providing an environment that allows both parties to identify and articulate their grievances and move towards an agreed way forward. Mention that you will be using a tried-and-tested framework, which will prevent the process from going off track and will benefit both parties.

With conversations like this, confidentiality is extremely important and you must emphasise that you will not pass on the details you hear in the discussion to anyone outside the conciliation process, unless you make a specific agreement with them that you can.

Once you have explained the way forward, get both parties in their individual conversations to commit to engaging in the process of conciliation.

From this potentially highly charged situation, see if you can get them to focus on specific behaviours, rather than just describing the events. As you actively listen, take copious notes and try not to judge, apportion blame or act as an advocate for either person. During this initial session your aim should be to 'boil down' what might be a heated, rambling and critical stream of consciousness into something that they can agree are the main issues.

Listening and questioning skills are essential here. Summarising regularly will also help to check understanding. More than any of the other conversations we have talked about, this is about looking at a person's energy. Are they animated or worked up, or flat with an air of resignation? Each situation requires a different skill. The animated person needs to be calmed and focused, whereas the quieter person needs to have the issues teased out of them.

Once I was working with someone who came across as hostile. Realising that if I left it without comment we would not be able to go on with the meeting, I simply said, 'Are you alright?'. Then she told me all about her situation and the things that had been happening to her recently that were making her beside herself with anger and causing hurt feelings towards the other person. Once she had shared her concerns, she was able to focus on the key issues.

The actual problem and the presenting problem can be very different. For example, they might say: 'They just keep changing the arrangements and then say that I don't take the initiative'. When you ask them to be more specific, they say: 'I just don't know where I stand with him. I set up the meeting last Wednesday and then on Tuesday afternoon he announced to the whole office that the venue had been changed and he did not even tell me about it.'

As you listen to both sides of the story individually, it is likely that you will warm to one person more than the other or believe one interpretation over the other. This reaction may be nothing to do with the behaviour or events as they are described. It might be that you have a similar communication style to one of the people, so can build rapport more quickly. You must take responsibility for any potential biases and realise that your role is not to take sides or decide who is right, but to act as a neutral witness to the events and move them through the conciliation process.

The best way to get to the core of the issues is to listen closely to everything that is said, write copious notes, while maintaining eye contact and stimulating them to talk more by saying things like 'Is there anything else?'. What you do not want is to get to the next stage and for them to say: 'Something I forgot to tell you when I met you was ...'. Most people, even very annoyed ones, run out of steam at some point.

Your aim here is to get as much information from the other person about what they perceive to be the problem as you can. If they are going on or rambling, steer the conversation a bit. Say things like 'Yes, I think I have got that' and do a brief summary. Alternatively, refer to something relevant that they said earlier that you want to pick up on, for example: 'You mentioned earlier that you disliked the way that your fellow director just cut across you when you were talking. Would you like to say a bit more about that and how it affected you?' The art here is to listen to what they have to say, while working out your next question and without disturbing the flow of what you are being told.

Alongside your own potential for bias, be aware of the individual's tendency to want to get you to agree with them and their explanation of events. The slightest hint of partiality will alienate the other person and threaten the integrity of the conciliation process. Listening is in itself therapeutic, and you will be surprised at how much of the emotional charge will dissipate simply by allowing them to tell their story while you listen.

During this stage, your intention is to assist them to identify and clarify the issues, which will be shared with the other party during the next stage of the process. In this phase, summarise regularly and reflect back to them what you perceive to be the key areas of concern.

Once you have heard their side of the argument, you will probably have lots of notes, which you will not have had the opportunity to assimilate. Take a few minutes to gather your thoughts and extract the key patterns and issues from the discussion.

Then report your assessment back to them, by saying something like: 'From what you have said, your main concerns are: 1. The levels of support you received from the other person. 2. The constant need to provide highly detailed reports, which prevents you from getting on with the work that you consider to be the main purpose of the role. 3. The pressure that they put on you to do things that make you feel uncomfortable. 4. Their tendency to circumvent you, and to go straight to your manager.'

When you talk to the other party in the same way, they might highlight a different set of reasons for the breakdown of the relationship, for example: 1. The lack of attention to detail. 2. A reluctance to do what is expected or asked of them. 3. Their constant need for reassurance and a lack of ability to use their initiative. 4. A lack of respect for their authority. 5. A change in behaviour since they got promoted or moved into the role.

Their reasons for the dispute may be a mirror image of the other party's or they might have a completely different perspective on the events that have occurred. At this point it would be worthwhile to ask both parties what would be an acceptable outcome to the conciliation discussions. This will help you when you come to explore with them the options to improve the situation.

Once you have agreed the key issues individually and created a workable agenda, which both parties can agree on, talk to them about how they will explain their concerns during the conciliation meeting. The process of identifying the issues should in itself have calmed both parties and takes the emotional charge out of the situation. Encourage descriptive language, which focuses on behaviour, not emotions.

Having heard all the issues and prepared the agenda, you should now be ready to bring both of them to the conciliation meeting. When they first meet, it is possible that the parties involved in the conciliation may feel uncomfortable even looking at each other. As you work through the stages, play close attention to body language and look for what conciliators call the 'golden moment', when the parties in dispute start to look at each other and engage in the process.

Stage 2: Hear the issues

At this stage, it is the conciliator's job to help the aggrieved parties to express their concerns and to hear the concerns of the other party. This should be done in a structured way and should reflect the more focused agenda agreed after the individual meetings. It is likely that one person will have prompted the conciliation more than the other, so it makes sense to start with their concerns. Always have a logical reason for who goes first in the conciliation process.

The conversation can be fluid or highly structured; this will very much depend on the style and skills of the conciliator. Personally, I feel that structure reduces the risk of the meeting going off track. Outlined below is a suggested three-step structure for Stage 2 of the conciliation process.

- **Step 1: Describe the key issues**
  Person 1 to express their issue without interruption from person 2.
- **Step 2: Comment on the key issues;**
  Person 2 to comment on person 1's statement of the issues without interruption;
- **Step 3: Hold a dialogue**
  Person 1 and person 2 to respond to each other's statements and dialogue about the issues raised.

During this stage your role as conciliator is crucial. You have to guide the conversation and listen to the issues at the same time. This is what I call 'dual processing'. You are listening in the present to what they are saying and you are trying to anticipate where you will guide the conversation next, without trying to control the conversation or use it to achieve an agenda of your own. Simple phrases like 'Go on' or 'I can see that you find this difficult, are upset or are concerned about the issues' can go a long way. Regular summaries after key stages can also be particularly helpful and can move the conversation along.

Try also to manage the time or the number of agenda items that each party has to tell their side of the story and establish this at the beginning of the meeting. Otherwise the hearing of the issues itself can often mirror the problem that one party perceives themselves to have more power over the other. Realise too that your personal biases will be working overtime, since you are likely to agree with or like one person more than the other. Be aware of this and make sure that every intervention you make is impartial. The moment one of the parties suspects bias or favouritism is the moment when the process can lose its integrity.

Once they have explored all of the issues and heard the other person's perspective, it is likely that the emotional charge between them will have been reduced once again. This will mirror and build on the emotional reduction process that occurred when you met them individually. If this is the case, you should be able to move the meeting on to the next stage, which is exploring the options. If one or other of the parties seems reluctant to do this, you might need to explore the concerns further and also to remind them that when they first began talking to you, they did agree that they would participate in the conciliation process.

Stage 3: Explore the options

Once each party has heard the other person's point of view, they have a number of choices:

- to walk away
- to continue to attack
- to come to some kind of agreement.

Since you have already contracted with them to engage in the conciliation dialogue and they have agreed to the meeting, it is unlikely that they will walk away. They may continue to attack, but often people's fears about what the other person thinks of them is worse than the reality. This is particularly true when their concerns have been explained in a clear, concise and structured way, rather than as emotional and erratic streams of consciousness.

Although you could get them to take turns to suggest options, it is likely that by now the conversation will be much more fluid and constructive. Your role as conciliator is to guide them towards identifying options, not to suggest them, evaluate them or select the way forward. If you do this, you may think that you are helping the process, but in fact you are interrupting it. There is no point in walking away from the meeting with a perfectly worded solution, if neither party owns the agreement nor feels inclined to implement it when you leave.

Again, people's approaches are different, but I think a legitimate part of the conciliator's role is to get all of the possible options on the table before they select which ones are going to be useful to them. Obviously, if they have agreed on the way forward and done this quickly, you would be getting in the way by keeping the exploring option process open, but while they are still reviewing them, it is always worth asking the question 'Is there anything else you could consider?'. This intervention often prevents the discussion going off at a tangent later.

Write down all the options and reiterate them so that they can jointly agree the way forward. Check with them that there is a basis for agreement. If there is no potential for agreement, depending on the situation you either need to keep looking for further options or move forward on the basis that there are no options available to improve the situation.

When you have facilitated this stage as fully as possible, you are ready to move on to Stage 4: making agreements.

Stage 4: Make agreements

Here you need to remember that it is not **your** agreement – it is the agreement of both of the parties. Your role is to make notes, perhaps to clarify what they say and to record what they agree. Once you have done that and ensured that both have copies, your responsibility in the conciliation process has come to an end. It is up to them to act on the agreements and change their behaviour, if they choose to do so.

An alternative method of reaching agreement during the joint meeting is to take each item on the agenda and explore the problem and the solution to the problem as you go along. Choose the method for you, which feels logical, leads to joint problem solving and is easy to explain to the participants in the conciliation process.

I have explained the conciliation approach rather mechanically here, because it is important that you understand the process very clearly before you start to relax the way in which a disagreement is managed. People in dispute are usually upset or angry, and your boundaries must be very clear at all times. To maintain your boundaries you need to:

- be impartial
- tease out the areas of conflict
- listen to concerns, but focus on the issues
- use a structure to work towards helping the parties to identify solutions.

Try not to go for a more informal approach straight away. Conciliation is a serious business and usually means a lot to both parties. Treat the seriousness of their concerns with respect. Aim for an approachable formality.

Once you have mastered the framework and achieved some successful outcomes, your style will relax naturally. But even then, never lose sight of the gravity of the conciliation role. At the level of conciliation, the skills are very subtle and although the conciliator may act as a catalyst for change, it may be virtually impossible to see them doing it.

As I have mentioned before, I believe that most people – if they apply the right beliefs and have the right skills – will be able to move up the continuum of interpersonal skills. The opportunity to acquire these skills is also a factor of the life experiences that we are exposed to. While I believe that your life experiences will get richer and more challenging as you develop more skills, realistically the number of people who have all of these skills will get much smaller as people nudge up the continuum. In fact, I would guess that in a population with relatively sophisticated interpersonal skills, there might be only a few thousand or so people who can operate at the level of conciliation.

Reactionnaire

What are you beliefs about becoming an effective conciliator?

What are your thoughts on the conciliation skills that I have covered in this chapter?

What feelings did you experience as you read the information on conciliation that was covered in this chapter?

What ideas 'popped into your head' as you read through the conciliation skills?

What actions are you going to take as a result of reading the section on conciliation?

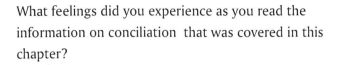

Top Tips to become an effective conciliator: see page 184.

Chapter 9
Taking a Stand

The Continuum of Interpersonal Skills – Taking a Stand

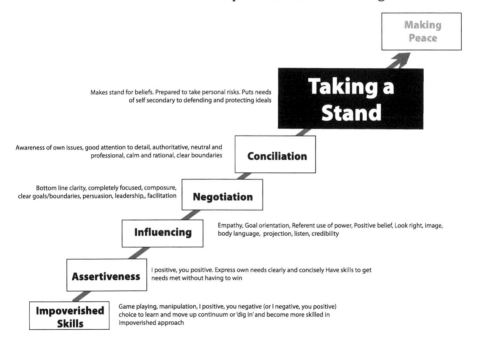

Seeing the continuum of interpersonal skills unfold with my clients so many times, I became curious to see if there were any other levels above developing the skills of conciliation.

Working closely with my long-term coaching clients and keeping a constant eye open for what areas they might move into next, I noticed that something interesting appeared to happen. When people have very high-level interpersonal skills and know they can get their needs met, and can assist others to get their needs met appropriately and with integrity, they tend to come 'out of the shadows' to make a stand for something that they believe in.

I have no idea why this is the case, but I have seen it often enough to believe that it is part of the process. It is as though they know they can achieve goals in a very subtle manner, but realise that at some point they have to have the courage of their convictions to make a stand. Here they are not talking or trying to persuade; they are letting their actions speak for themselves.

This stage is typified very well in the film Jerry Maguire, in which Tom Cruise plays a successful sports agent who, almost against his better judgement, writes a paper on how the business should be run along more ethical lines. He does this despite knowing that his views will be highly unpopular with the management. As a result, he resigns. After some very clear 'What have I done?' moments, he is able to demonstrate some pretty fancy negotiation and conciliation footwork in order to set up and build a successful value-driven business.

Although I had sensed that this stage existed, it took me ages to find the right language for this behaviour. Whatever I came up with – from 'direct principled action' to 'standing up for your beliefs' – it seemed to miss the essence of what this level is about. Then some of my clients with excellent interpersonal skills started to behave in this way too. Although they could achieve most of the goals they set themselves, they were deciding that they could no longer work within their current organisations or systems, and were 'taking a stand for what they believed in'.

At this level, their actions involved either physically leaving the environment or making unpopular decisions, which they knew might risk their future. When reaching this point, I have seen people leave organisations suddenly, when they feel that there is no longer a 'fit' between their values and the values of the organisation. If they decide to stay, they use their new understanding of themselves and how they operate to speed up the changes they want to make within their environment.

Value-driven behaviour

Up until this point, I think that people are driven by inherent values and beliefs. But at this level, it is almost as if the values become actively dominant, and then these values start to be tested. I do think it is odd that this happens. Why would someone who has an excellent track record, and who has achieved everything they want to achieve through exceptional interpersonal skills and a sense of focus, suddenly throw it all up in the air to take a stand for what they believe in? What seems to happen is that they realise they have real power, which they can use either to benefit themselves or to improve the human condition. There is also a possibility that these people, who are very secure in themselves, may just want to know what would happen if they did make a stand.

Although our beliefs and values drive our behaviour, we rarely articulate them. When coaching a board-level client, I was talking to him about a dubious decision he had been asked to commit to. Although clearly part of him was intrigued by the challenge and the skills he would need to have to 'pull it off', from his turmoil around the decision, I also sensed that it was affecting him at a far deeper level. So I asked him what he stood for. Now this is not an easy question for most of us to answer and although we have a guiding compass, we rarely make these unconscious drives conscious. By a process of elimination and comparison we identified his values. What struck me was how useful those values would be in determining the correct action for him in the future. In other words, he would not need to have sleepless nights deciding what he should do in any given circumstance. Instead, he could use his moral compass to help him make the decision.

I also worked with another very successful, very value-driven client. When faced with working in an environment whose values were at odds with his own, he suddenly left the organisation. Such apparently erratic behaviour becomes much more common – and even predictable – when people have reached the point of making a stand for what they believe in.

So how would you know you are here, and how would you identify your driving values and beliefs? Well, first you will sense a deep sense of unease and you will probably not know why you feel that way. You may even tell yourself that you should toe the company or party line. But somehow you are just not able to do so.

If you feel this type of unease and you have acquired the other skills, whether you want to or not, you are likely to be on the verge of taking a stand. When working with clients at this level, I have found that common patterns of expressed values are:

- fairness
- believing that they are on the side of good
- wanting to work with others who share their goals
- being prepared to take a stand for what they believe in
- producing information with integrity
- making decisions for morally justifiable reasons.

Transparency in our values is often prompted by an event or a series of events, which test our unconscious sense of right and wrong. Conscious awareness of our values can then be used to speed up our decision-making process and help to maintain and deepen our sense of self. This inner moral compass can be particularly useful when the going gets tough.

This is demonstrated by a story a client told me. He admired the way a colleague dealt with the politics in his organisation. He took risks, and very much enjoyed the tussle of negotiation with other departments and outside organisations. My client asked him how he managed to do this, and he said he always took the view that he was well motivated, played with a 'straight bat' and did things for the right reason. In other words, he allowed his strong sense of values and knowing what was right to drive his actions.

Your values might be whirring away in the background, but it is only when you are driven to make a stand about them that you realise how much, or how little, they mean to you. Although we act on our values all the time, we rarely expose them to ourselves. It is only at the stage of 'taking a stand' that your values seem to become an integral part of you and part of your personal decision-making process.

So how do you make unconscious values conscious? This is not an easy question to answer. A very simple and common indicator of emerging value-driven behaviour, at this level, is a deep sense of unease about something that is happening around you. When this happens, take a step back and consider which of your values are being challenged.

When I was writing this book, I also experienced a series of incidents that made me consider my own values more closely. Firstly, I had been talking about writing the book for a long time, and in the end one of my very kind friends said to me, 'Pam, either write the book or shut up'. This made me think about what was stopping me and I realised I was concerned that: the book might not be good enough; my approaches were not sufficiently original; I would not be a good writer; and other people might criticise my ideas. It is also an awful lot of typing, it takes time to organise your thoughts and tremendous discipline to sit down at your computer for hours on end, not knowing whether you will get to share your ideas with all the people who could benefit from them or whether your work will be consigned to the publisher's 'slush pile'. My head kept on trying to put me off writing the book, but my heart would not let the issue rest. In the end, the frustration of not writing the book far outweighed the discomfort and possible risks of writing it. From this decision and the other incidents that happened around the same time, I realised that my values were: wanting to share my ideas, 'walking my walk, talking my talk';

fairness; consistency; respect for others; leaving situations I felt uncomfortable in; and not wanting to be manipulated.

When you are aware of your values, commit them to memory and use them to evaluate your concerns the next time you feel uneasy about a situation.

Dreaming the dream

Taking a stand for what you believe in might also be when dreams become reality. I am a huge believer in dreams and our power to attain them. I have this belief because I have seen dreams played out in people's lives many times. They can be hugely effective in guiding our working lives, providing we take the time and trouble to pay attention to them.

My favourite story about a dream occurred when I was managing a career centre, which had been set up to support hundreds of customer service staff whose jobs were being relocated. With the help of professional CVs, advice on the job search and assistance with interview practice, most of the employees were getting new jobs mainly in the same line of work.

Despite the success of his colleagues, one very capable supervisor stood out because he was not getting the jobs he was going for. Since I was able to meet this man on a number of occasions, I had got to know him well. He was highly personable and, in addition to assisting his colleagues with their job applications, he had arranged for agencies to come in to his workplace to sign up his team. During this time we also chatted about his interest in investing and financial matters.

After his third unsuccessful interview for a customer service role that completely matched his skills and experience, it occurred to me that he might not be getting the jobs because he did not want them. I reflected this observation back to him. At this point his shoulders slumped and he admitted that this was true. I decided to realign his CV to reflect his knowledge and interest in financial matters and told him to use his considerable interpersonal skills to approach some banks and building societies directly.

The next time I met him, he had been interviewed for a customer service role in a well-known building society. At the end of the interview they said, 'We like you, but we are not going to offer you the job'. They then interviewed him again and asked him to do a presentation for a job at the next level up in the organisation. Again they said they liked him, but were not going to offer him the job. A few weeks later he came to the centre and he was delighted – the building society had interviewed him for an even more senior position and had given him the job. They had recognised his talents and, despite his having no previous experience in the field, had decided to take him on as a deputy branch manager. I went to visit him in his new role a few months later, and he told me that he loved the job and had waiting lists of people wanting to speak to him about their mortgages.

Feeling very smug about my suggestion that he approach financial institutions directly, I asked him if he had done that and he said no. What had actually happened was that he had walked into his local building society, where he was a regular customer, and the woman behind the counter had said 'Do you want a job?'. He had said 'Yes I do, but how do you know?' and the woman behind the counter said: 'Well, you never normally come in during the week'. At this point he was not only able to pursue his application, but he was also able to present a highly professional CV, which reflected his knowledge and passion for financial services. I do believe that when you commit to a particular course of action, events often happen which move you closer to achieving that goal.

Once you start to become in control of your life and your behaviour, lots more goals start to become possible. Things that were previously out of the realm of possibility start to become within your reach. Dreaming the dream is the flip side of having negative beliefs. These are beliefs that you can achieve whatever you want – within the realms of your experience and expertise.

If I sound hopelessly optimistic, it is because my own experience and work with clients has taught me to be this way. As far as I can see, it is all about expectations: if you expect little from life, that is what you will get. If you expect a lot from life and you take action to move towards your goals, you will find that your dreams start to become possibilities.

A few examples prove my point. I was once working with an organisation where some pretty uninspiring characters were going to be approaching the job market. One young woman almost shouted at me, 'Well I don't want a low-paid job'. I thought for a minute and replied that she would only get a low-paid job if she applied for one; so if she wanted a higher-paid job, she should only apply for those positions that paid the type of salary she was looking for. This sounds obvious, but it is amazing how many people set their sights low and are then surprised when they achieve them.

Equally if you set your sights high you are more likely to reach those goals, if you believe you can achieve them and have the skills to help you get there. Here is an example of this approach from a friend of mine who worked with people with learning disabilities. He had recently taken on a resident with no bodily movement apart from an ability to blink. After a few weeks of working with this man, my friend wondered if the blinks meant anything. Slowly but surely he and his staff were able to work out that the resident was able to communicate via the blinks. Can you imagine how much more of the world opened up for this resident, once they discovered this link between his blinks and his needs and desires? This realisation not only made the staff excited to communicate with this man, but also curious to know what other hidden depths existed in the other clients that they worked with. My friend believes that people have capacities far beyond what is expected of them, and then he sets out to find the evidence that this belief is correct. When people constantly prove him to be right, this reinforces his belief.

Another example of setting your sights high and achieving them comes from a coaching client of mine. I worked with her for a year and each of the monthly sessions was taken up with dealing a different member of staff who had not been managed properly in the past and had adopted chronically bad work habits. I remember the first session very clearly as she described a person who came to work but sat down and did not really do anything productive all day. Interspersed between her comments about the woman's behaviour she kept on saying 'she's not a silly woman'. Picking up on these remarks I suggested that my client give her a task she might have to do herself but this woman could do instead. As soon as I said this she mentioned that she had been meaning to do a newsletter and that she could ask this member of staff to do it. She did ask her to do the newsletter and it was such a success that the woman received some very positive feedback. She then asked my client if there was anything else she could do, beginning a gradual rehabilitation back into becoming a useful member of staff.

When people work in a demoralising and demotivating environment even the most motivated people can 'switch off'. It takes a very dedicated and aware manager to reignite their enthusiasm. When I looked back on the year's coaching with this particular manager I commented on the fact that unusually each of the sessions had been taken up by devising strategies to find a 'spark' in a different member of staff. All of these staff members had clearly been part of what turned out to be a particularly motley bunch. I will never forget her reply as we were reflecting on our work together and the progress of her team members. When I mentioned that she had some very difficult staff to manage, she just simply said, "It's all I have!"

My client had a tremendous belief in people, which was reinforced with each success she had in turning the behaviour of a member of staff around.

The best story I ever heard about dreaming was from a colleague, whose client was a senior accountant and said he wanted to be a chief executive. In view of his skills and the downturn in the job market, this desire seemed unachievable to my colleague. So my colleague encouraged his client to put the dream to one side and concentrate on finding another senior accountancy role. About a year later, my colleague bumped into him on the golf course and asked how he was getting on.

He said: 'Great, I achieved my goal of becoming chief executive of a company. Then I decided that I only wanted to work three days a week. Now for the other two days I play golf.' When most of us hear about dreams that do not fit in with our own view of reality, we have a tendency to laugh and criticise the person who has the dream for being unrealistic. In fact, from my experience, the more you visualise alternative futures and take the active and realistic steps described in this book, the more likely you are to achieve your dreams.

A friend recently asked me why I wanted to write this book and I told her this story. When I first got into the people development business, I was very passionate – some would say idealistic – about helping people become more effective. I attended a seminar on ethical marketing, to increase the number of people I could sell my services to, and had the opportunity to have a masterclass with the facilitator. I told him how I wanted to use my skills to have an impact on the world. He listened patiently, then asked me a couple of questions: 'You work in London, don't you? How many organisations do you think there are in London?' I have no idea about numbers, so I said: 'Oh, about 350,000'. He then asked: 'OK, how many people work in those organisations?' I said: 'Oh, about 4 million'. He then said: 'With the best will in the world, how many of those do you think you can train?' Through a few simple questions he demonstrated to me that at that point in my career, I was not able to have the impact that I desired. That one exchange put things into perspective, and for the next 17 years I concentrated on doing the best possible job for the thousands of people who did cross my path.

So I went away and refocused my work to help the individuals and small groups I came across to be more effective in their working lives. During this time, with the help of my clients, I kept learning, observing, making patterns and creating assumptions about human behaviour. I tested out the ideas I have outlined in this book to check their effectiveness and validity. On many occasions, people also gave me valuable insights which enabled me to explore my thinking further, and suggested other levels of interpersonal skills that might be apparent. It was an evolving process that enabled me to develop people with a greater degree of predictability and success. I now believe that I have the skills and expertise to achieve my original dream: to help a wider audience of people to become more effective and in control of their working lives. So the dream never did go away – it just became submerged until it was ready to be revisited again.

As you start to achieve your goals and gain more control of your life, you will realise that you have dreams. You will also begin to appreciate that those dreams can be fulfilled with not too much effort on your part. So open up your mind and learn to love and live the dream.

Reactionnaire

What are your beliefs around your ability to take a stand
for what you believe in and 'dream the dream'?

What are your thoughts on the taking a stand for what
you believe in and 'dreaming the dream' ideas that I have
covered in this chapter?

What feelings did you experience as you read the
information on taking a stand for what you believe in and
'dreaming the dream' that was covered in this chapter?

What ideas 'popped into your head' as you read through
the chapter on taking a stand for what you believe in and
'dreaming the dream'?

What actions are you going to take as a result of reading the section on taking a stand for what you believe in and 'dreaming the dream'?

Looking at the goals you set out on page 10 of Chapter 1, *The Wisdom of Patterns*, what progress are you making towards your, six month, one year, ten year and life time goals?

What stops you from achieving these goals.

Top Tips to taking a stand: see page 185.

Chapter 10
Making Peace

The Continuum of Interpersonal Skills – Making Peace

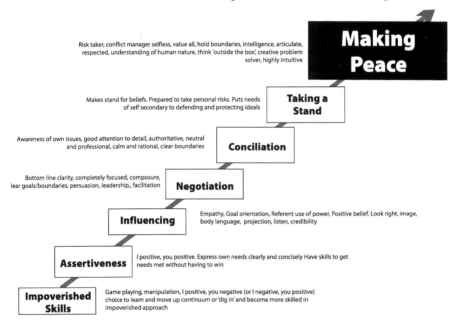

Although I believe that making peace is the ultimate goals of the continuum of interpersonal skills, I have not reached the level where I am making peace – and nor will most people you will come across. Few individuals have the necessary commitment, application or opportunity to develop their skills to this point.

There is, however, a very small (but growing) number of people who are achieving successful outcomes for peace on the world stage. In this section I want to explore some of the current thinking on peacemaking, to review the beliefs and skills displayed by these high-level negotiators and to examine the implications for development required to achieve exceptional results against formidable odds.

The beliefs of the peacemaker

Below are some quotes from some of the world's significant peacemakers. As you read them, notice the common pattern: first, there is a sense of being called to take action; second, there is a sense that they have the skills to make a difference; and third, they have a belief that peaceful outcomes are achievable.

George J Mitchell, US Senator who headed up many all-party talks in Northern Ireland:

'I was in a position to help. I didn't seek or expect it, but it was a reality. How could I turn away from it now? I had been taught that each human being has an obligation to help those in need; I had preached the same thing to young Americans countless times. Did I really believe what I said? And if I did leave, and the war resumed, how could I reconcile myself to the deaths that would result, deaths that might have been prevented if I had stuck with it?'

Source: *Making Peace* (William Heinemann 1999)

Jonathan Powell, Tony Blair's Chief of Staff and Principal Adviser on Northern Ireland:

'So if there is one lesson to be drawn from the Northern Ireland negotiations, it is that there is no reason to believe that efforts to find peace will fail just because they have failed before. You have to keep the wheels turning. The road to success was littered with failures. And there is every reason to think that the search for peace can succeed in other places where the process has encountered problems – in Spain, in Turkey, in Sri Lanka, in the Middle East, in Afghanistan, and even in the longer term with Islamic terrorism, if people are prepared to talk.'

Source: *Great Hatred Little Room: Making Peace in Northern Ireland* (Bodley Head 2008)

Michael Young, Public Affairs Director of Consolidated Gold Fields (a British mining company in South Africa) and facilitator of the peaceful transition to majority rule in South Africa:

'I took the view that there was only one issue, and it was "How do you get from a rigid, totalitarian, white-driven state to a black state through the process of the ballot box?" I suppose for me that was partly driven by an intellectual exercise but it's also fair to say I was the licensed liberal in the mining house.'

Source: *Extract from an interview with Michael Young broadcast on the Channel 4 website, 25 April 2009*

What these people have in common is a **belief** that they can achieve a different outcome in combination with the high-level **skills** to enable that outcome to happen. All of them have achieved their goals through mobilising community leaders, building trust and using a clear process to build bridges between people with very different political perspectives.

Although it would be inappropriate and premature for me to suggest a step-by-step process which encourages all of us to go out and negotiate peace deals, I think it is worth exploring what Michael Young (who successfully facilitated the peaceful transition to majority rule in South Africa) called his 'template' for peace. This process was later adopted in Northern Ireland. His template for peacemaking was to identify key players in the political arena who were serious, but not necessarily visible, and then to create an environment where they could meet and begin to understand each other as human beings away from the spotlight.

The invisibility of the peacemaker

In 1985 Michael Young was Public Affairs Director of a British mining company in South Africa, Consolidated Gold Fields. In this role he was responsible for formulating long-term strategy to protect the company's interests in an increasingly volatile and violent society, which disenfranchised the black majority through the practice of apartheid.

In an interview in 2009, **Michael Young** said of his role in the peace process:

'You have to believe in what you are trying to do. It is important that people should know that I had a very particular view on the hopelessness, uselessness and evil of apartheid.

'But it is not good enough to believe that something is evil – you have to actually get to rationalise and say what can I do with my skill set in the area in which I operate to do something practical to change it.

'So there is an impetus, then there is the rather, cold, analytical, hard nose set of propositions used to work through what is feasible.

'We needed to take the process away from the theatre – it needs to be a silent process – if you want to give it a real chance for something positive to happen. You need to bring people together and remove the potential for playing to the gallery. You have got to get them to understand one another as human beings. In the process I began to chair the sessions in a very strong way, in a directional way, and as the colleagues black and white began to work together as South Africans, I could and should and did pull back and took on a much more passive role, as they began to take ownership of the process. And once that began to happen I really did believe we had some traction.

'I tend to believe that my best work is done quietly; I don't need to have a high profile to function. It doesn't get me out of bed in the mornings.'

Source: *Extract from an interview with Michael Young broadcast on the Channel 4 website, 25 April 2009*

Seeing his job as 'thinking the unthinkable', Michael Young was challenged by Oliver Tambo, co-founder of the African National Congress (ANC), to set up a dialogue between the ANC and the Afrikaner establishment. In response to the invitation, Young persuaded his company chairman to take the considerable risk of allowing the talks to take place in secret in England, without the knowledge of the board.

Then he went on to convince key players to jeopardise their personal safety and security, by inviting them to take part in an overtly political but intensely secret process.

The meetings began with Thabo Mbeki, the exiled leader of the ANC and Professor Willie Esterhuyse, an Afrikaner, social reformer and philosophy academic. Meeting on 12 occasions between 1985 and 1990, the talks gradually involved more key players, including (towards the latter stages) President FW De Klerk's brother Willem.

Although there was a clear agenda for the meetings, Young took advantage of the intimate setting provided by Mells Park House in Somerset to create opportunities for the participants to meet outside the formal negotiations. He maximised the opportunity for chance conversations, by giving opposing sides adjacent rooms, encouraging walks in the grounds and creating a comfortable atmosphere with superb food and whiskey during the rest periods.

As they relaxed and got to know each other as human beings and fellow South Africans, they stopped being opponents with radically different beliefs and started to build trust. Outside the formal negotiations, as they felt safer in each other's company, Young would withdraw to create the space for them to talk. This environment of trust eventually led to agreement to negotiation without preconditions.

Although it is clear that he was acting out of humanitarian motivations, not just commercial interest, Young also hints that he regarded it as an intellectual challenge. Having been an adviser to Edward Heath and having worked with the British Foreign Secretary in the Foreign Office, he had the political acuity and exceptional interpersonal and problem-solving skills to achieve remarkable outcomes.

What is different in this case is that Young was prepared to believe that a radical and peaceful solution was possible and to take the huge personal risks to test whether that belief could become a reality. He also had a template for peace, which he wanted to test out during the negotiation process. The regular, formal, residential meetings created a fertile ground for the informal meetings. In the formal peace talks, the meetings had agendas. Outside the meetings, the informal agenda was to allow the warring parties to learn to see each other as people rather than opponents. It was this regular contact, and the encouragement of dialogue outside the formal process, which enabled the trust to develop. When the trust emerged, the real movement in the negotiations occurred.

Interestingly, this process was mirrored in Northern Ireland. In his book *Great Hatred, Little Room: Making Peace in Northern Ireland* (Bodley Head 2008), Jonathan Powell makes a number of observations as to why peace succeeded in 2007 where for three decades negotiations had failed. Although he suggests that a change of leadership created the political will to believe that a negotiated agreement was possible, he also infers that having a 'functional process' and keeping it going regardless of the difficulties was the key to success.

Initially, in both Northern Ireland and South Africa, leaders of the opposing parties set out preconditions to a negotiated settlement. In the case of Northern Ireland it was weapons decommissioning and in South Africa it was the release of all ANC prisoners. It seems that entering into talks with preconditions makes the parties feel safer and protects them against their opponents in the first instance. In fact, when trust had been built and they negotiated as equal human beings, the successful talks were held without preconditions in both instances.

Readiness to get around the negotiating table is crucial to the peacemaking process. Jonathan Powell gives credit to Gerry Adams and Martin McGuinness members of the IRA delegation for being prepared to 'break out of the blinkers', and suggests that over the course of the negotiations both became increasingly sophisticated politicians. In the case of the ANC, it was the co-founder Oliver Tambo who suggested that talks with the Afrikaaner establishment should be initiated. So establishing a willingness to talk is critical to the success of a peace process.

Both of these agreements took years. At the end of the process not only was a workable solution negotiated, but all parties could also be seen to be shaking hands, relaxed in each other's company, smiling for the camera and making jokes. Commenting on the previous failed 1974 Sunningdale agreement, Seamus Mallon, the former SDLP Deputy First Minister in Northern Ireland, asked if the permanent May 2007 agreement was just 'Sunningdale for slow learners'. In other words, had it taken over 30 years for the political climate to change, for party leaders to emerge who were prepared to talk, and for someone with a belief in the possibility of a negotiated settlement to consistently and persistently back a peace process? And finally had the main protagonists developed the skills to enable them to make peace?

It is possible that during these long, protracted talks, with a clear process and a belief in making possible the apparently impossible, these highly skilled facilitators gradually and subtly passed on their exceptional interpersonal and processing skills to the main parties in the negotiation. In other words, during the long, protracted negotiation process, which took place over a period of years, the opposing parties managed to move from a position of 'I positive, you negative' position, to a 'You positive, I positive' position. Once their beliefs about the value of the other party had shifted, they were able to develop their assertiveness, influencing, negotiating and conciliation skills to successfully navigate through the peacemaking process.

Throughout this book I have proposed that at each level up the continuum of interpersonal skills there is a step-by-step approach, which can be learnt and copied to achieve exceptional and repeatable results. This approach has to be combined with a **belief** that the outcome is both possible and desirable. When researching people who make peace, it is easy to get swept up in the charismatic and heroic nature of their achievements and to lose sight of the fact that what they are doing has a similar and predictable quality to it.

Successful peacemakers believe that they can make a difference. They believe in themselves, believe in others and believe that people – given the right circumstances – are basically honourable. They also believe that they have the skills and ability to create an alternative world view.

The skills of the peacemaker

In terms of their skills set, peacemakers tend to have:

- a calm centre, which enables them to resist all attempts to goad them into angry or defensive reactions
- the determination to take a stand on a particular issue
- frameworks to create dialogue
- an ability to negotiate, slowly, incrementally and systematically towards agreement
- a long-term view (they often negotiate over a period of years)
- an intellectual understanding of the key issues
- a strategic mind
- a remarkable ability to remain impartial, even in the face of huge pressure to take sides
- a strong sense of their own boundaries
- a resistance to game-playing and being drawn into disputes
- an ability to focus on the task and the process simultaneously
- an ability to put the needs of the peace process above a desire to gain personal recognition
- a readiness to approach the parties involved in the disputes as people
- the patience to take an extraordinary amount of time to build trust
- in the midst of often complete hatred, the ability to build rapport, establish their credibility and convey to people that they are people worth doing business with
- an ability to listen for clues, which indicate a party's desire to settle and move their position during the negotiation process

- the patience to enable the process to unravel naturally
- a balance between maintaining momentum, while not pushing towards action
- a natural curiosity to see if they can achieve agreement from an intellectual perspective
- the ability to put the needs of the peace process above their own needs for security.
- As you will have noticed, I have a tendency to form patterns about human behaviour and to use these patterns to assist people to improve their interpersonal skills. While it may be too early to form a model of peacemaking from these two situations, I think what is emerging is a very new and highly skilled approach to conflict resolution. From personal reflection, I thought I would be presumptuous and outline the steps that I observed in these two peacemaking situations.

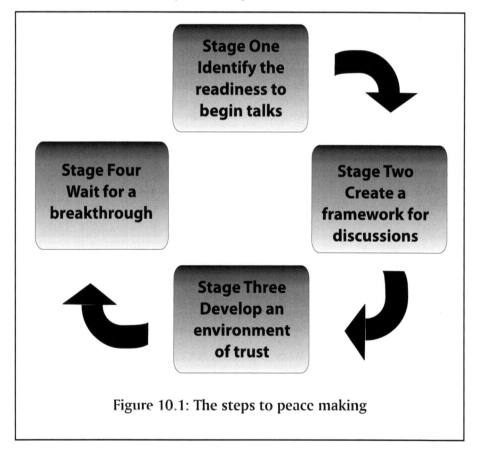

Figure 10.1: The steps to peace making

1. Identify the readiness to begin talks.
2. Create a formal framework for discussions and keep the momentum going away from the spotlight.
3. Develop an environment of trust. Create opportunities for the protagonists to get to know and trust each other as people.
4. Wait for a breakthrough.

Now this sounds highly simplistic, and of course it is: but only those people who have developed all the skills on the continuum of interpersonal skills will be able to achieve successful outcomes. This is a highly skilled business with not inconsiderable risks for the people who decide to take on these challenges.

The Continuum of Interpersonal Skills

One colleague, a Doctor of Professional Practice, summed up the complexities and satisfaction of developing peacemaking skills wonderfully.

All attempts to express the complexities of human interaction are partial but this 'continuum of interpersonal skills' is more inclusive than most. This articulation of a model that is simple enough to fit on one page yet subtle enough to support the lifetime task of developing interpersonal skills is an attractive recipe.

There is choice offered throughout and the language used is supportive and optimistic. The positive consequences of moving through the continuum are self-evident.

We are beckoned by Pamela to build our skills to enable us go beyond our own points of view and communicate effectively with other human beings to the point that we can manage conciliation.

And then we are prompted to consider that conciliation may simply provide a welcome and soothing balm. Peace making, on the other hand, is based on deeper understanding, of self and other, and thereby holds a stronger possibility of being sustained. The learning steps after conciliation wisely encourage the student of life to stretch beyond any potential mediocrity, challenging the reader to achieve the clarity that comes through taking a stand. It is on this sound footing of knowing where one is in relation to the issue(s) of the day that one is able to plan for peace.

Making peace is not a task to be achieved, once and for all, but with the skills and desire one may be able to gain and sustain the ability to continue as a peacemaker.

Reactionnaire

What are your beliefs around the possibility of developing a template for peace?

What are your thoughts on the peacemaking process covered in this chapter?

What feelings did you experience as you read the information on peace making that was covered in this chapter?

What ideas 'popped into your head' as you read through the chapter on peace making?

What actions are you going to take as a result of reading the section on making peace?

Top Tips to becoming a peacemaker see page 186.

Chapter 11

Defusing the Arch-manipulator

So far, I have presented a highly optimistic view of using effective interpersonal skills to achieve your goals and dreams. I have done this because my own experience and the experiences of my clients have taught me that these techniques are effective.

I mentioned in Chapter 4 that impoverished interpersonal skills and game-playing cause many of the problems between people, and I have pointed out that the skills I set out in this book will neutralise most of the negative or manipulative behaviour that you may come across. However, even some of my clients with highly developed interpersonal skills have problems in dealing with people who have exceptional (and apparently well-practised) skills for creating chaos in their organisations – the arch-manipulators.

Most manipulation can be spotted with some basic underpinning knowledge of assertiveness. However, these characters are different. Their influence is very subtle but powerful. They create chaos where none existed before, set departments against departments and generally tie the organisation up in knots. Usually my coaching role is to assist clients to develop strategies to streamline their operations, influence at national level or overcome resistance to progress. But they also need to understand the behaviour and motivations of a type of person who seriously, and apparently deliberately, undermines what has already been achieved.

How to recognise an arch-manipulator

From listening to my clients who were experiencing problems with these difficult people – or arch-manipulators – they appeared to share some common factors. They were often highly charismatic characters who appeared out of nowhere with no formal recruitment process in place. They sometimes claimed overseas qualifications and experience, but due to the lack of formal recruitment process and the sense of authority they commanded, these claims were often not checked.

The arch-manipulator appeared to create chaos that had people running around in circles and erupting in emotional outbursts, while this person sat back and watched it happen. They often made their interventions in the name of greater efficiency, proposed new structures because the current ones were not working, and suggested that people were not doing their job properly. When all the tasks were allocated, they rarely had a significant project or chunk of work to do and they cloaked all of their contributions in terms of the authority gained from their patron or other person in authority. While their contributions were incredibly general, their criticisms were very specific and they would get the most even-tempered of people swinging into action to defend themselves.

In other words, they knew what buttons to press to create chaos and they appeared to take a great deal of pleasure in walking into a room, pulling the pin on the hand grenade, then stepping back to see the result of their actions.

These people seemed to have an ability to identify my clients' personal 'Achilles heel' or weak spot. They seemed able to exploit those areas in such a way that normally calm and collected people started working harder, protecting their backs, arguing with people they usually got on with, defending themselves and building arguments to resist apparently illogical decisions.

Once you start to notice the behaviour, it is very tempting to look for motivations behind it. While it is true that it could hide some kind of malpractice, the most likely reason for this behaviour appears to be power or to look more intelligent than they feel they actually are. Arch-manipulators love to identify how they can wheedle themselves into an organisation and gain huge satisfaction from manipulating it, just because they can.

They also appear to have a 'hold' on the leader of the organisation or group, although they seem unlikely to go for the leadership role itself. When you begin to realise what is happening, it is tempting to wonder why the leader does not observe it too. It might even cross your mind that the arch-manipulator knows something about the leader that would embarrass them if made public. I think it is simpler than that: I believe that they use the same skills on the leader that they use on everyone else. In other words, they play into their insecurities, then use this reflected, unappointed or unelected power that they have gained to destabilise the organisation.

The strategies of the 'Controversial Dialectician'

One of my clients became interested in the strategies of powerful men. He told me about a publication called *The Art of Controversy* – Volume 5 by Arthur Schopenhauer[7], who (writing in 1831) described a form of interaction called 'the Controversial Dialectic'. This is defined as the art of disputing, and of disputing in such a way as to hold one's own, irrespective of whether or not you are right.

In this extended essay, Schopenhauer identified 38 common tricks and dodges used by people who he perceived lack the learning, intelligence and self-respect to present their case in a logical, reasoned, truthful, just and yielding manner.

The 38 stratagems that Schopenhauer set out for winning arguments can be paraphrased as follows.

1. Exaggerate then discredit the opponent's position.
2. Pick out a word or phrase which stands out, then misinterpret it.
3. Attack something different from what was asserted.
4. Conceal the game, by gradually gaining admissions and then mingle premises and admissions into the conversation.
5. Draw a true conclusion from a false premise.
6. Discredit truth, by making sweeping generalised statements about the subject area in general.
7. Ask a number of wide-ranging questions at once, so that people will not notice gaps or mistakes in the argument.
8. Make the opponent angry, so that he is incapable of good judgement and of perceiving where his advantage lies.
9. Put questions in a different order than the conclusion to be drawn from them requires.
10. If someone continually says 'no', ask the question in the opposite to get them to say 'yes'.
11. Use support for particular cases to suggest support of generalised cases.
12. Use phrases, words or metaphors which suggest a positive interpretation of the preferred position.
13. Give an exaggerated and less favourable view of a counter-proposition.
14. When the argument is not going their way, claim victory anyway.
15. Suggest seemingly absurd propositions from the opponent's arguments.
16. Say the equivalent of 'If you are not happy about the situation, why don't you do something about it (e.g. leave, resign, speak up)?'.

---

7   The Pennyslavia State University – Penn State Electronic Classics Series 2005

17. If the opponent presses counter-proof, advance a subtle distinction.
18. Interrupt, break or divert a successful line of enquiry.
19. If pressed to find an objection in a winning argument, make a generalised criticism of the human condition.
20. Draw final conclusions yourself, even though some of the premises are lacking.
21. Counter superficial and misleading arguments with equally unsound arguments.
22. Create a circular argument, where the conclusion appears both at the beginning and the end of the argument.
23. Irritate your opponent into exaggerating their argument through contradiction and contention.
24. State a false deductive argument.
25. Identify a single instance to the contrary to overturn their argument.
26. Turn their opponent's arguments against them.
27. If an argument accidentally causes anger, press the point more to exploit the weak spot.
28. Use ridicule and laughter against an opponent, to get the audience on your side.
29. If the argument is being lost, create a diversion.
30. Appeal to authority or universally held opinion, rather than to reason.
31. Declare a lack of understanding of the opponent's argument.
32. Link their opponent's argument with an 'odious' category or 'ism'.
33. State 'that is all very well in theory, but it will not work in practice'.
34. If a weakness is identified and reduces them to silence, press the point more.
35. Demonstrate that the opponent's viewpoint is contradictory to their self-interest.
36. Puzzle and bewilder, by blasting with words assumed to have meaning.
37. Refute a faulty proof to a correct argument and use it to discredit the whole position.
38. Become personally insulting and rude.

As you can see, the whole premise of the Controversial Dialectic is 'I positive, you negative', so it is essentially an aggressive stance. I have included these stratagems not to suggest you learn them, but to make you aware of their existence. Once you realise you are dealing with someone who likes to indulge in this type of interaction, you can prepare some more considered responses.

At a very primitive level, as human beings we are programmed to defend ourselves or attack the opponent if threatened. Faced with the very sophisticated and skilled stimulus used by a very tiny proportion of the population, people with highly developed interpersonal skills find themselves either defending themselves or attacking the other person. This may involve doing masses of additional work that we know is unnecessary, or justifying our actions for reasons which we cannot quite explain. Alternatively, we become very emotional or angry, despite all our efforts to control our reactions.

Imagine you are a highly skilled individual who considers that you can always get your point across in an intelligent, considered and structured manner, which most people can understand and accept, even if they do not always agree with you. Then you come across one of these characters who seem to have a way of deflecting and reframing everything you say to the detriment of your argument. I believe it is only natural to think that these people are highly intelligent, because mostly you do not feel flummoxed in this way. You will then feel that you are missing something and must just concentrate more. It is precisely this level of surprise, shock and disbelief that lets practitioners of the Controversial Dialectic get away with these approaches. It may take a while for you to realise that whatever you say or do, you are not going to 'win', because you are not in an environment where logic or rational thinking has any relevance. You can then decide not to play the game, despite the very strong invitations you are receiving to engage in this behaviour. Once you are aware of the existence of this phenomenon, you can create your own strategies to deal with it.

What amazes me about this list of 38 stratagems is how predictable these ways of winning an argument are and that a group of people exist who consistently and systematically use these techniques. At the end of his essay, Schopenhauer suggests that unless you wish to play this game with someone whose intelligence and integrity you respect, the best way of dealing with people who like to engage in the Controversial Dialectic is to allow them to say what they please, since 'everyone is at liberty to be a fool'. He also quotes Voltaire, who said that 'Peace is worth more than truth' and an Arabian proverb, which says: 'On the tree of silence there hangs its fruit, which is peace'.

From working with clients who have successfully disengaged from playing this game, it is clear to me that in line with the assertive approach the most effective way to deal with these strategies is not to respond to them. This is much easier said than done, since people who learn these strategies are extremely skilled in the art of deflection and enticing people into debates that they are unlikely to win.

Strategies to defuse the Controversial Dialectician (or the arch-manipulator)

In order to disengage from the chaos that might be created in the environment by these techniques, I suggest you take the following actions.

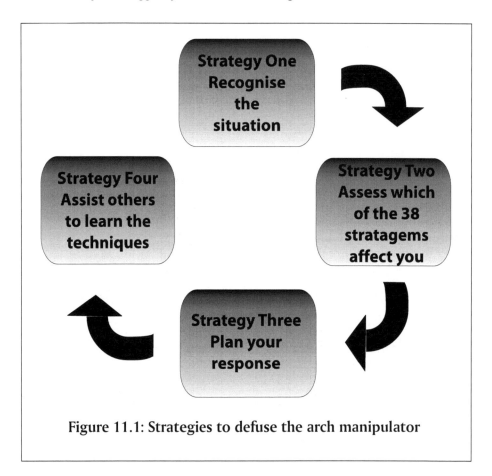

Figure 11.1: Strategies to defuse the arch manipulator

1. Recognise that this very rare situation might be happening

The first priority is to spot and identify the situation. This can be quite difficult when you find yourself surrounded by chaos that did not used to be there before. Do not try to convince other people of its existence. Defuse it yourself and then you will be in a strong position to assist other people to defuse it too. Be careful not to jump to conclusions over isolated incidents.

2. Assess which of the 38 techniques the Controversial Dialectician might affect you personally

Arch-manipulators have a tendency to disempower you and disconnect you from your own sense of logic and integrity. Notice what 'buttons' they can press within yourself and others. For one client, it was his need to control his temper and his tendency not to take criticism well, combined with his compulsion to defend himself. For another, it was his need to maintain an audit trail of everything, so that he was able to defend against any criticism; this engaged him in spending valuable time putting in back-up systems and justifying his actions. For another, her personal standards meant that he only had to criticise a small element of her performance and it would send her into self-doubt and additional work.

Now this might not sound that bad, but imagine that the person with these skills is able to find the 'weak spot' for anyone in the organisation. So it would not be long before they are all dancing to the tune of the Controversial Dialectician, rather than to the tune of the organisation and its goals.

This tiny group of individuals appears to like tying people in knots. They will plant little triggers in conversation, letters and emails, which will be almost unnoticed by others, but will have you reacting in the way they expect.

They encourage you to make long explanations of the reasoning behind your behaviour, then criticise your logic. They will bury an almost imperceptible insult into their response that you feel forced to address. Then they will hook onto your unreasonable and irrational behaviour, and start to imply that you are not fit to do the job. They will copy other people into your communications and suggest an implied criticism from you of another person. This will start you communicating with this third party directly and either defending your behaviour or attacking theirs, when before the email you were interacting just fine. They will be aware that you are under deadline pressures and will imply that their work is more important and that you should drop what you are doing. In other words, they gradually and subtly start taking over your working life and your thoughts.

I think you get the general idea. So what do you do if you have a person like this is your midst? The simple answer is: do not feed the behaviour.

3. Plan your response to resist the very powerful desire to react to the stimulus that you are receiving

Now this is going to sound easier than it actually is, but you need to stop using defending or attacking behaviour in response to their stimulus. From the assertiveness toolkit (see Chapter 5), broken record, fogging and negative assertion are still the most powerful techniques to keep you on course and avoiding deflections.

For example, if they have noticed that you tend to get drawn into the game when you are criticised, instead of long explanations which can be broken down piece by piece, give vaguer answers that suggest that everything is under control. When you are personally criticised, use fogging statements, which suggest that you can understand why they may say that. In fact you do understand why they might say that, of course, because you believe that they might be manipulative or unhinged. Go back and re-read Chapter 5 on dealing with deflections. The issues are the same, but because of the more subtle and pervasive challenges presented by the arch-manipulator, who tends to work at senior levels in organisations and groups, you might be knee-deep in chaos before you step back and consider what has changed in your environment.

I hope you get the picture. The moment you start dancing to their tune is the moment when you will get caught up in the whirlwind. So slow down, take a step back and review their behaviour and the way it is affecting you. Then stop reacting the way you have been doing. Generally become a bit more vague and unavailable.

The more you can learn to regain your control, the more you will help others to do the same.

4. Assist colleagues, friends and family to identify the situation and to learn the techniques to disengage from the game

When you have managed to disempower the Controversial Dialectician and regained your sense of control, it is likely that others will become curious about how you managed to defuse the effects of the manipulator in your midst. You can then share your strategies with them, to enable them to do the same.

In the cases I have worked on, when these tactics have been identified and defused, the inefficiency, incompetence and dishonesty of the protagonist is revealed. When they have lost their power, after a while most arch manipulators will move on to another organisation or group, where they can again become the centre of attention. In fact, after a while, people hardly notice that they were there or have disappeared, and start instead to refocus on the goals and objectives of the organisation.

When I shared this chapter with the client who prompted me to read Schopenhauer's *The Art of Controversy*, he responded that he considered that the greatest success he had had with his own particular arch-manipulator was when he responded to an email that was a rant and tirade of threats which contained many Controversial Dialectic hooks by replying: 'I am sure he will do whatever he thinks appropriate'. He then went on to say that he had not experienced a reoccurrence of the problem since. He also commented that he thought that this response sounded very similar to 'fogging' in the assertiveness toolkit.

A final comment on manipulative behaviour: it is very important to realise that some behaviour has a positive impact while other behaviour has a negative impact. Mostly we learn our behaviour or personal stance early on in life. Not all of what we learn is ultimately good for us. I hope I have shown that habitual learning can be unlearnt. When I talk about defusing manipulative characters, I am not talking about changing them – you are just stopping their behaviour from having so much power over you. Whether we decide to adopt different behaviours to achieve different outcomes is a personal choice. Of course, I would hope that when manipulative behaviour ceases to have a pay-off, people might decide to re-evaluate their stance towards others, particularly when they notice that direct, open, more authentic communication can achieve more effective results for them.

The darker side of power

The arch-manipulator brings me to an interesting point that many of the people I coach raise, either when we start the skills development process or towards the end, when their skills are quite sophisticated and subtle.

I mentioned at the beginning of this book that the skills of the arch-influencer or the arch-manipulator are the same; the only difference between them is the intention of the person who uses them. In the end, I think you have to learn to trust your gut instinct on who you believe is working for you and who might be frustrating your process in some way for their own motives. In fact, people who know the power of these skills may wonder if it is ethical to describe these strategies, when they can so easily be used for the purposes of manipulation. My argument against this view is that people who have a tendency to manipulate are constantly improving their skills. When they learn to do something and it works, they do it again and then look for the next technique they can use to flex their power base or acquire assets that they value. You will notice that this is a similar process to the one I suggest you adopt in this book in order to progress up the continuum of interpersonal skills.

In a way, manipulators have been able to rely on the rest of the population (who they regard as a bit dim) not to suspect their intentions and motivations. I consider teaching these skills to be an equalisation process, to enable the people who do not have a tendency to be manipulative to get their needs met.

In the process of learning these skills, you will also be able to spot and defuse people whose motives seem less than honourable.

Reactionnaire

What are your beliefs about the existence of arch manipulators?

What are your thoughts on the process suggested to defuse the impact of arch manipulators?

What feelings did you experience as you read the information that was covered in this chapter?

What ideas 'popped into your head' as you read through the chapter on the impact of arch manipulators and how to defuse them?

What actions are you going to take as a result of reading the section on defusing the arch manipulator?

Chapter 12
My Soapbox

As I finished writing this book, I asked myself why I had wanted to write it.

Of course I wanted to share my knowledge about techniques that I know work and have changed the lives of thousands of people. I wanted them to be available to a wider audience than I had previously been able to reach. I also wanted to check whether models and ideas that I explain to people quite simply in a coaching environment would have the same impact if people just read about them without the one-to-one intervention.

Having given the manuscript to a number of people who I thought might benefit from it, the results are very promising. People have changed significant factors in their lives, and have started to adopt new and more effective behaviours.

While this is great to observe, I also have another motive, which is much more personal. I love to chat with people who feel in control of their lives, like to develop others and add value to society. I think this leads to greater creativity and to discussions about improving the way that the world should be.

Most of the people I coach stay in contact with me and we become friends. I would like to grow more friends who I can have a chat with and encourage others to grow like-minded people, who they can also have a chat with. It is only when more people have the skills described in this book that we will be able to achieve a more peaceful society and a more peaceful world. If that sounds a bit prosaic, remember that acting out of a calm centre, being more creative and achieving synergy through collaboration with people is far from dull. It is just a different way of looking at life.

I hope that as you have read the book, you have tried out some of the techniques and approaches I have suggested and have shifted your ideas about what is, and what is not, possible in your working and personal life. I also hope that you have swelled the ranks of those people who feel that they can make an impact in their lives and make a contribution in the wider society.

After reading this book, if you think you need further assistance, seek out an assertiveness course, or find a mentor or coach to help you to develop your skills in this area. Alternatively, complete the exercises in the *People Skills Revolution Companion Workbook* (2011) that is designed to help you explore in more detail the ideas outlined in this book. To get you started the first few chapters have been included at the back of the book (see page 187) to enable you to consider your negative beliefs and develop your assertiveness skills. I can almost guarantee that whether you are a chief executive of a major organisation or whether you provide your services directly to a customer, these strategies will teach you something about yourself and others that you did not already know.

As a development consultant I have always been attracted to personal development, rather than organisational development. One reason for this is that, having worked in many organisations going through significant change, what strikes me is the importance that personal agendas play in what actually happens, compared with what is planned to happen. Often, personal needs and agendas are met to the detriment of the overall vision, strategy and objectives. Also, much of the organisational development budget is wasted on initiatives that have little chance of success.

I can give a good example here. I was doing appraisal training in an organisation where, although people left the course feeling enthusiastic about the process, it was clear that the organisation was not supporting the initiative in any way. Feeding this view back to the organisational development manager, I told him that I felt he was wasting his investment due to the lack of support. In response he asked me to carry out a review of the appraisal system within the organisation. Talking to managers and staff at every layer, in groups and one-to-one, it was clear that there was a lot of support for the process at a grass-roots level, but there was a block somewhere. Finally I facilitated a meeting with the senior managers working directly for the chief executive and it became clear to me, that regardless of what others in the organisation wanted, the senior managers were blocking this initiative. In other words, they were taking the 'I positive, you negative' view. They considered that they knew better than any of the other staff what was best for them. Until their lack of belief in the system was addressed and they developed the skills to conduct successful appraisals, the organisational blockage in the system would have remained.

I have also observed highly successful transformation programmes unravel when a new chief executive wanted to be liked and could not say no to requests that were off the project plan. Equally, departments seriously overspend when no one is prepared to negotiate priorities and costs or to take the necessary steps to work within the agreed budget.

On the international stage, aggression is also common, as representatives of countries play the 'My country is better than your country' game. From the peace negotiations I have described in Chapter 10, it is clear that this 'I positive, you negative' stance has to change before any serious progress can be made. Moving up the continuum of interpersonal skills is a process, which can increase the number of people who are capable of making peace. But – and it is an important but – it is not just about attending a course or adopting a new set of skills, it is about living the experience of learning to identify, and act consistently with, your values on a day-by-day basis.

It is my belief that lack of confidence and low self-esteem are rife in organisations, on the international stage and in society generally. It is about time someone said 'The king has got no clothes on and told the truth'. Until we acknowledge this, we are all victims of mass media, marketeers, politicians and bullies at work and home who feel that their needs are more important than our own. In the process we lose touch with, or maybe never even got to know, our true selves. In its place we are being encouraged to consume more to feel good about ourselves. 'Keeping up with the Joneses' has become a national pastime. This seems like a good enough game, until you realise that the Joneses are probably struggling to feel good about themselves, just as much as everyone else.

This lack of a calm centre within us often allows others to take advantage of the situation to achieve their personal agendas. Because I believe that assertiveness underpins all the interpersonal skills that I have described in this book, I would encourage decision-makers to invest their finite resources in developing these skills – not just for those staff working directly with clients, but for all staff from factory floor to boardroom. When running assertiveness courses in a work setting, the most common piece of feedback I receive after the workshop is, 'I wish I had known about all of this years ago'.

I would encourage the teaching of assertiveness in schools to start building the skills early and to ensure that this momentum is maintained in the workplace.

Investing in assertiveness throughout the population would create a common language and enable people to spot and defuse those individuals who may not be working in our best interests. From experience, what will happen almost naturally is that people will start to influence with good intention, leading to quicker, more effective decisions, greater autonomy, increased creativity and 'thinking outside the box'.

Should I be worried that this book will help manipulators to hone their skills? I do not think so. Manipulators develop their skills naturally. They try an approach and it works, so they repeat it. They then look for the next technique that they can use to get other people to do what they want. The continuum of interpersonal skills is simply an invitation to use this skills-building approach, but in a positive way and with integrity.

If you invest your time and money in building on your interpersonal skills, you will release the incredible energy and creativity that lie within yourself and others, which are at present being blocked – by people themselves (with their own negative beliefs) and by others who believe that it is not in their best interests for everyone to get their needs met in a clear, direct and straightforward manner.

By supporting the development of interpersonal skills, starting with assertiveness, you will be empowering yourself and others to believe that better outcomes are achievable. You will also reduce the game-playing and the widespread manipulation that can cripple organisations, groups, families, and countries, since people will also have a common language to defuse the behaviour that deflects them from their path, or disables them from achieving the most favourable results.

At the beginning of the book I mentioned that someone had asked me if I really am this optimistic or just naive. You are also probably wondering if everything can be quite as simplistic as I have described it. Well yes, I am probably being naive. I have made it all sound very simple, to inspire you to change your world one step at a time. The problem, if you can call it that, is that I **do** see the world that way, and once I have that filter on, I find it difficult to take the filter off. Why should I want to do that?

For me, the continuum of interpersonal skills is very real. It is the way I interpret the people and the world around me. I have used it to develop my own interpersonal skills, to identify the next level up the continuum and to help other people increase their skills too with considerable success. It is my belief that when more people start to develop and use these skills consciously, that the world will become a more peaceful, productive, lighter and more enjoyable place to live.

Top Tips

Achieving a People Skills Revolution

1. Notice situations when you would like to be more assertive.

2. Make the decision to become more assertive.

3. Adopt an 'I positive, you positive' stance in your interactions with others.

4. Decide what different outcomes you want to achieve.

5. Anticipate what 'hooks' people may use to deflect you from your purpose.

6. State your aim clearly and concisely in a logical manner without becoming emotional or using language with an emotional content.

7. Practise using the techniques of broken record, fogging, negative assertion and negative enquiry in low risk situations.

8. Recognise that it will take time to feel comfortable with the approach.

9. Realise that in the first instance you may feel guilty especially if you have a need to be liked.

10. Give feedback and praise in a clear, concise, and timely manner.

Tops tips to become more influential

1. Get to know the people you want to influence and then present your request at a time and pace that matches your relationship.

2. If you only learn and apply the skills of building rapport and none of the other skills outlined in the book you will find that your confidence increases significantly.

3. Use Carl Jung's model of psychological types: Intuitor, Thinker, Feeler and Sensor, to understand yourself and others better and to communicate more effectively.

4. Influential people do not just establish their credibility when they first meet a new person or group; they do it at any point when they need to increase their impact and remind people why they should listen to them.

5. If you want to influence someone, you must frame your comments in the light of their agendas, rather than the agenda that might be of most interest to you.

6. It is much harder for people to say 'no' to a request when you have just spent the last few minutes chatting to them.

7. Do what you promise to do and thank people for what they do for you to create goodwill which will enable you to continue building on the relationship the next time you meet them.

8. Magic occurs when you chat with people. Use chats to bring your thoughts to life, stimulate your creativity and transform your ideas.

9. The power of chats is fuelled by becoming an effective listener and questioner.

10. Practice influencing skills everyday until you become a 'natural'.

Top tips to become an effective negotiator

1. Everything has a value – you just need to work out what the negotiation is 'worth' to you. Successful negotiaton is as much about having a positive outlook combined with the basic interpersonal skills and treating the other party with respect as it is about learning technical moves and strategies.

2. If you want to be an effective negotiator you must get over any negative thinking you have about your ability to negotiate.

3. Take your time to prepare and learn the stages of negotiation: prepare, debate, propose and bargain and be clear about what stage you are in at any given time.

4. Before you can begin to play the negotiation game you have to understand the rules.

5. When planning your negotiation strategy have as many 'wants' as you can realistically generate.

6. Ask yourself the question ' Is there a deal to be done here?' by looking at their clues and assessing the other party's energy and engagement in the process.

7. Make all offers conditional using an 'if you do this, I will do this' format.

8. Keep track of what you are proposing and make a note of their response.

9. Test the boundaries and parameters for areas of possible agreement.

10. Effective negotiation is the meeting of minds of two equals, ensure that you use the skills responsibly.

Top tips to become an effective conciliator

1. Integrate the skills of assertiveness, influencing and negotiation.

2. Develop a relationship of trust.

3. Have a clear framework to work within – identify the issues, hear the issues, explore options and make agreements.

4. Be open about the process.

5. Act in a highly confidential manner and listen to their grievances individually in order to tease out the key issues.

6. Assist the participants to translate emotional events into described behaviour.

7. Be aware of and minimise the impact of potential bias in favour of one of the parties.

8. Use assertiveness techniques to prevent parties from moving away from the agenda.

9. Act as an impartial witness at all times.

10. Move the parties respectfully through the process and encourage joint problem solving.

Top tips to taking a stand

1. Ask yourself the question 'what do I stand for?'

2. Consider the last time you had to make a heart over head decision – what did your choice say about your values?

3. When you feel uneasy about something that is happening in your environment take a step back and consider which of your values are being challenged.

4. Trust what your heart is telling you over what your head is telling you.

5. When you are aware of your values, commit them to memory and use them to evaluate your concerns the next time you feel uneasy about a decision.

6. Align your skills behind your dream.

7. If you expect a lot from life and you take action to move towards your goals, you will find that you dreams start to become possibilities.

8. Set your sights high, believe you can reach them and develop the skills to get you there.

9. The more you visualise alternative futures and take the active and realistic steps described in the book, the more likely you are to achieve your dreams.

10. Revisit the goals you set yourself on page 10 and review what progress you are making towards your 6-month, 1-year, 10-year and lifetime goals.

Top tips to become a peacemaker

1. Integrate the skills of assertiveness, influencing, negotiation, conciliation and taking a stand.

2. Believe in the ability to create an alternative world view and have the high-level skills to make it happen.

3. Identify the key players who are serious, ready but not necessarily visible to come to the peace table.

4. Create an environment where the protagonists can meet and help them to understand each other as human beings away from the spotlight.

5. Think the unthinkable and believe in the apparently impossible.

6. Have a formal, structured process and keep it going.

7. Take the long term view.

8. Subtly develop the interpersonal skills of all the protagonists.

9. Create an environment of trust by leading by example and encouraging conversation and building of relationships outside the formal peace process.

10. Believe that it is possible to make a difference, have self belief, believe in others and believe that people – given the right circumstances – are basically honourable.

Annex 1

Exercising Your Interpersonal Skills

Having read the introduction and sections on changing negative beliefs and assertiveness, use the following exercises from the *People Skills Revolution Companion Workbook* to explore these issues in the context of your own work and personal life situations.

Optimist or pessimist?

Our belief system plays a central role in how we see the world and our ability to impact on it.

Are you generally an optimist or a pessimist about your ability to impact on people and situations around you?

What influenced you to adopt this pessimistic or optimistic outlook?

What effect does this outlook have on your life and the outcomes you achieve when interacting with other people?

What phrases or statements did your family or educators use to suggest what you would become or what your life would be like?

How have these phrases or statements impacted on the way you behave in your working and personal life?

Reflection: Sometimes it is not easy when we identify the link between the way we were raised and our behaviour in adult life. Consider the answers you have just given and reflect on what they mean to you. What reactions did you have to doing this exercise and how did your responses make you feel?

Remember: *'Whether you believe you can, or you believe you can't—you are usually right'*. Attributed to Henry Ford.

The Continuum of interpersonal skills

The continuum of interpersonal skills model suggests that once people become more assertive, they naturally progress on to become more influential, interested in negotiating and take on a more conciliatory role. A smaller percentage of people will also go on to take a stand for what they believe in and become peace makers.

What reactions did you have to the Continuum of Interpersonal Skills model?

What do you think is the logic behind this approach?

Reflection: What do your answers suggest about how useful the approach will be to you.

Remember: Writing in 1936 Dale Carnegie, in his book *How to Win Friends and Influence People*, talks about research conducted by the University of Chicago into what adults want to study. The survey revealed that health was the prime interest for adults and that their second preoccupation was people – 'how to understand and get along with people; how to win others to your way of thinking'. People's concern about understanding themselves and how to get along with others remains as true today as it was over 70 years ago.

Adopting positive beliefs

When people perform below the standards they set themselves, more often than not they have a negative belief about their ability to achieve different outcomes.

Think of the last time you performed below par. What was the situation, who was involved and what happened?

Did your behaviour in this situation reveal any negative beliefs that you have about yourself?

How might these negative beliefs affect your ability to impact on situations like this in the future?

Identify one negative belief that emerged as a result of looking at the situation you have described for example ' I can't do this', 'people don't listen to me', 'people don't like me', 'I might as well not be there', ' I will be rejected' and write this down.

What internal reactions does this cause you to have?

Given the negative thoughts in your head (internal reaction) relating to your negative belief, how do you perform when you are with that person or are in that situation? How is your performance interrupted?

When your performance in front of someone has been interrupted due to your absorption with your own negative thoughts about your how well you are doing, what do you come away thinking, which would confirm your original negative belief?

If the situation has not happened yet, but you have negative beliefs and thoughts about it, use the model to imagine what you think might happen.

Reflection: When you surface your negative beliefs and their associated internal reactions it can be quite shocking to discover that you have these thoughts and feelings about yourself which affect your ability to impact on other people and situations. Now take a few moments to consider the answers you gave to this section. Write down your reactions to the comments you made.

Remember: You are not creating these internal reactions. You are just shining a light on them to become more aware of the impact that they have on your performance. When we have negative beliefs and internal reactions about ourselves, these tend to intrude when you are with other people either on a one to one basis or in a group. Although you are physically present your mind can be absorbed by observing (and usually criticising) how you are performing with the result that less of your energy is available to be involved in interacting with the person or people in front of you.

This process can explain why we can get drawn into a downward negative spiral about ourselves and our ability to impact on certain situations or people. In fact, after a few circles around this process, you might start to generate other more destructive negative beliefs.

Beliefs are the result of where we decide to focus our attention and you can start the process of thinking more positively just by selecting a more positive belief around a person or situation

Selecting positive beliefs

What would be a more positive belief in relation to the person or situation you have just described? (Be sure that the statement is wholly positive and does not include any negatives.)

What internal reaction would you have towards this person or situation, if you held that more positive belief?

If you held that belief and you had that internal reaction, how would you imagine yourself performing when you were with the person?

If you have imagined the way you would be in your performance with the other person correctly what would you walk away thinking about the encounter that you have just had?

If all of the above reactions were actually true how would that affect your belief about that person and situation?

What impact would achieving a more successful outcome in this situation tend to have on your ability to impact on other situations you currently find challenging?

Consider what other negative beliefs you have about situations and people

Negative beliefs you have about your ability to interact with others

1._____

2._____

3._____

4._____

5._____

Either repeat the exercise above to explore your negative beliefs and how they impact on your internal thought process and your performance

OR

Reframe each of your negative beliefs to be more positive about your ability to achieve different outcomes.

Revised positive beliefs you have about your ability to interact with others

   1._____

   2._____

   3._____

   4._____

   5._____

How would you feel about yourself and your ability to impact on other situations and people if you held these positive beliefs?

Reflection: On completing this section on adopting positive beliefs, what are your reactions to what you have written? Pay particular attention to any resistance or sense of optimism that you might be experiencing

Remember: The process of doing this exercise makes you feel more optimistic about approaching the interaction more positively in the future. The outcome may not be perfect straightaway but the process of adopting more positive beliefs will start the self-reinforcing cycle of achieving more effective outcomes

Impoverished interpersonal skills

Do you know anyone who you consider to be a game player, bully or a door mat?

What tends to be the outcome of their behaviour when interacting with others?

Considering the ideas presented in the book what could be a more positive interpretation of their behaviour, i.e. learnt behaviour, negative beliefs about themselves, not having skills to achieve different outcomes, having a bad day etc?

When might you have been guilty of this behaviour yourself?

Reflection: What reactions do you have to your answers regarding people who have impoverished skills?

Remember: Not everything that someone does is about you. Look after yourself and the relationship will take care of itself one way or another. We all have 'off days'.

Assertiveness: How 'I positive, you positive' are you?

Think about the 'I Positive, You Positive' position. Be honest with yourself, what is your natural tendency or dominant style?

I positive, you negative _____

I negative, you negative _____

I negative, you positive _____

I positive, you positive _____
　　　　　　　　　　　　　　(tick one)

What impact does this tendency to behave from this position have on your behaviour?

Would you say that you have a particular tendency to be passive (putting the needs of others before your own), aggressive (putting your own needs before the needs of others) or to swing between the two positions?

What comments about your impact on them have more than two people made about your interactions with them? Be sure to include positive as well as negative comments.

What patterns of comments, positive and negative, have you received from people about your behaviour?

Do you think there is any validity in these comments. If yes why? If no, why not?

What actions or changes in your beliefs about people would it take to shift your current position to be more 'I positive, you positive?

Reflection: It is not easy to reflect on who we are and how other people see us. We tend to see and hear comments, which reinforce our view about ourselves. Make sure your comments include all the positive comments that people have made about you and your impact on them. Then reflect on what your have learnt about yourself in answering these questions.

Remember: Some people may not know what their positive or negative stance is in relation to others. This is because our behaviour and the impact we have on others may be outside of our awareness. Patterns of comments from more than one person can give a good clue to how others see us. Individual comments about our behaviour can often be unhelpful and may just be 'hooks' that some people use, to deflect us off a course of action that does not suit them.

Give up 'stamp collecting'.

Stamp collecting is the process of collecting resentments about people's behaviour in the same way that you might have collected trading stamps in the past. When you have a full book you cashed them in for a reward. In the collecting stamps analogy the reward is the release of anger resulting from the built up resentments in relation to someone or the attention you receive for uncharacteristic behaviour.

Are you a stamp collector (building up small resentments which then blow up into a bigger disputes)?

What do you collect stamps about in relation to the behaviour of others?

Does a particular person or type of person trigger this reaction in you?

What effect does holding onto the resentment (stamp collecting) have on your behaviour and feelings?

What action could you take to avoid collecting stamps and avoid the situation from escalating?

Reflection: It might come as a surprise to you to know that you collect stamps about situations or people when you may consider yourself to be a very easy going person. What are your thoughts on the answers you have given in this section?

Remember: It is only when we are more aware of our behaviour and understand why we do things that we can begin to change our reactions to people and events. Awareness is the precursor to change, so although it may be uncomfortable to find out about some hidden aspects of ourselves it is exactly this process that enables us to make different choices in the future.

Identifying your needs

Sometimes it is easier to stop having needs because we do not have the skills to get those needs satisfied. In order to become more assertive we need to recognise and value our needs. For some people this might involve becoming reacquainted with needs that they gave up on a long time ago.

What are your needs? List three things that you know you need when interacting with others, e.g. to speak so that people listen, to be able to request a promotion, to be able to express your ideas, to be respected, to ask for things you want, to be able to act on your feelings.

1._____

2._____

3._____

How do you ensure that you get your needs met?

If your awareness of your needs is a bit shaky what could you do to become clearer about what they are?

What needs do other people have that you wish you had? This will help you to identify needs that you have but may not be aware of, such as being able to say 'no' when people ask you to change shifts, asking people to do something for you, or challenging people when they have done something you are not happy about

1._____

2._____

3._____

What would you like to change about your interactions with other people?

What specific words or phrases do people usually use to deflect you from your intention to get your needs met?

How do you feel when they manage to deflect you off your intentions and you feel that the same incident or event has 'happened again'?

If you do 'stick to your guns' and get your point across, how do you feel after the event?

Reflection: This can be one of the most difficult sections to complete since you may have to confront the thought that you stopped having needs because you lacked the skills to get your needs met. Reflect for a moment on your comments about identifying your needs and getting your needs met. What reactions did you have to doing this section and how did completing the questions make you feel?

Remember: We all have needs and have the right to get those needs met. The skills of assertiveness will give you the strategies to stop putting the needs of others before your own needs. Once you learn to do this you will start to re connect with your own needs and be able to develop the interpersonal skills to get your needs met on an increasingly regular basis.

The assertive tool kit

The basic assertive tool kit, includes the techniques of:

Broken record
Fogging
Negative assertion
Negative enquiry
Giving constructive feedback

Think of a situation you would like to change?

What more positive outcome would you like to achieve in this interaction?

How could you use the tools of assertiveness to approach this situation differently?

What could you say to state your needs without showing emotional behaviour or using emotional language?

With the situation you would like to change in mind, what 'hooks' would you imagine the other party might embed into the conversation to deflect you from your intentions to be assertive and achieve a better outcome for yourself?

Some common phrases to watch out for are:

Flattery

You are the expert in this field. No one will give me better advice than you can.

You have always been so reliable, friendly or helpful in the past.

I tell everyone how wonderful you are.

I know I can rely on you to help me.

Can you change your arrangements for me since you have helped me out before?

Criticism

If this is not done by this afternoon my job is on the line (or your job is on the line).

But there is no one else to help me.

I am relying on you.

You are being very aggressive.

I might have to report you, you know.

What do you mean you are not going to do it?

But I thought you were my ally.

You have to do it, it's got to be done today.

You do know your appraisal is coming up shortly don't you?

I am very disappointed in you.

List below what phrases or words you imagine the other person might use to deflect you from your intention to be assertive

Anticipated deflections

1._____

2._____

3._____

4._____

5. _____

Using the assertiveness techniques of broken record, fogging, negative assertion and negative enquiry, plan an assertive response to all of these statements

Anticipated response to deflections

1._____

2._____

3._____

4._____

5._____

Reflection: This section is about using tried and tested assertiveness techniques to achieve your goals and avoid being deflected off your path by other people. What are your reactions to using the tools of assertiveness in your own work or personal life situations?

Remember: Avoid giving background information, excuses, descriptions or offers that provide the other person with the opportunity to 'hook' onto what you have said. Giving too much information allows them to take control of the conversation and turn the discussion back onto their needs and agendas rather than yours.

Equally do not feel compelled to follow up or respond to flattering or critical remarks which are intended to deflect from your intention to get your needs.

People are much more predictable than you think. As a general rule, a person who wants to deflect you from your intention to become more assertive will usually use flattery and if that does not work they will criticise you.

Receiving criticism like this can be difficult for the person who likes to be liked and wants to be recognised as the person who does a good job. When working with clients who are improving their assertiveness skills they often feel they are not progressing when they get criticised when in fact the opposite is the case. To be criticised (when you are not usually criticised) suggests that the other person is beginning to notice your resistance. You have not responded to flattery and you are standing your ground more. Learning to deal with criticism is just part of the process of becoming more assertive and resisting what might be the unreasonable demands of others.

The moment you respond to one of these deflective 'hooks' and follow that line of conversation, is the moment that you have lost control of the interaction.

Overcoming feelings of guilt or unease

In asserting yourself it is likely that you will feel guilty at least in the first instance. Or alternatively you may not have got your needs met (when you usually do) because you have been assertive rather than aggressive.

How would you deal with these outcomes?

What would you do about feeling guilty?

What would you do about not getting your needs met in the way you have become accustomed to?

If you have had a tendency to be passive and have been successful in getting your needs met you may feel guilty. If you have had a tendency to be aggressive you may feel a sense of dissatisfaction when you have allowed others to get their needs met. What would be the benefits of living with these feelings of unease for a short while?

How do you feel about the possibility of getting your needs met when this might mean not meeting the needs of others?

How would you feel if you gave up getting your needs met in order to enable other people to express and meet their needs?

Reflection: Reflect for a moment on your answers. How do your answers make you feel?

Remember: Moving out of your comfort zone is by definition uncomfortable. Until you learn to do this your comfort zone will not expand. So sit with the discomfort for a while and know it will pass. All learning involves a degree of mental stretch and discomfort.

Giving effective feedback

Once you are successful in becoming more assertive you become less enmeshed in your own thought processes and begin to become more aware of the behaviour of others. Much of the less productive behaviour of others can be modified by using the assertiveness techniques described in Chapter 5. However when you start to notice that you are 'collecting stamps' in relation to another person's behaviour it is useful to give them constructive feedback rather than allow the build up of resentment to continue.

Who would you like to give constructive feedback to and why?

Be specific about their behaviour and how it affects you

What would you like to be different about their behaviour

Plan your conversation using the constructive feedback model
Make it recent, descriptive, factual, non-judgemental – (don't use labels)

Constructive feedback model

When you did this …………...…..

I felt or thought

And it had this impact on me ………..

Pause for discussion

What I would like you do next is

Because ……….. explain how this would improve the situation

When you pause for discussion, what are you going to say to ask them to comment on your suggestion?

When you raise this issue with them you are likely to get one of two reactions – either 'its not just me – the others do it too' or 'oh I did not realise'. What is their most likely reaction if you raised this issue with them?

Plan your response to their reaction to ensure that you are not deflected from your intention to give feedback.

What would you like them to do differently next time this situation arises?

How would this improve the situation?

What can you say to encourage them to comment on or discuss your suggestion?

Reflection: Giving constructive feedback to people can be challenging especially if you have not really done it before. How did answering the questions in relation to giving feedback make you feel?

Remember: A great deal of our own significant learning comes when someone has the courage to tell us something about our behaviour that we might not like to hear. Since most of us do not like to be told about the negative aspects of our behaviour and how it affects other people we have a natural tendency to try to deflect the conversation or change the subject. You need to anticipate what the other person might say to sidetrack this conversation. When you have this conversation with someone if you get stuck or side tracked go back to the model, work out where you were in the process and start again from there.

Next steps

Reflection: If you have completed all the exercises in this section of the book, on exercising your interpersonal skills, you will have covered a lot of ground and asked yourself questions you may never have asked yourself before. It can be very challenging to look at yourself in this way. What are your thoughts on the process you have just completed?

Remember: If you have completed these exercises and tried them out in real work or personal life situations you will have stablised many of your interactions with other people and gained more control of your time, resources and corporate or personal wallet.

You are ready to build on your new insights about yourself and to develop the more advanced skills outline in the book. This will enable you to achieve more positive outcomes in your work and personal life.

You have just completed the first sections of the *People Revolution Skills Workbook Companion*. I hope you have found the exercises useful. If you would like to develop your skills further, the *Workbook Companion* will provide a practical guide to developing the more sophisticated people skills outlined in the *People Skills Revolution*.

Annex 2

The Continuum of Interpersonal Skills Model

Over the page is a larger scale version of the Continuum Skills Model.

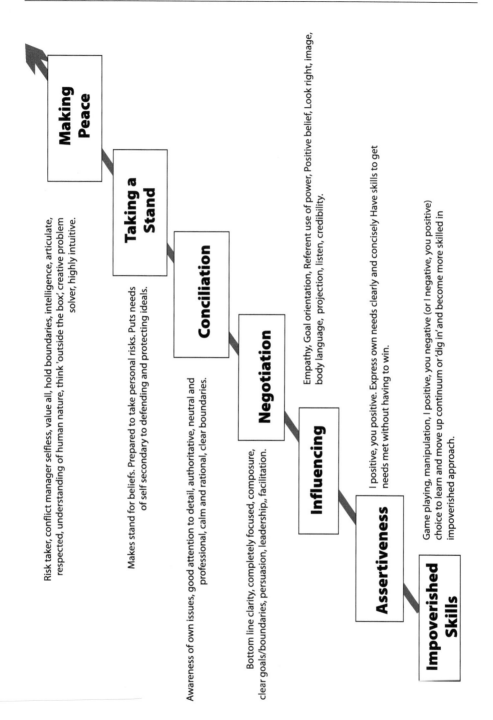

Making Peace

Risk taker, conflict manager selfless, value all, hold boundaries, intelligence, articulate, respected, understanding of human nature, think 'outside the box,' creative problem solver, highly intuitive.

Taking a Stand

Makes stand for beliefs. Prepared to take personal risks. Puts needs of self secondary to defending and protecting ideals.

Conciliation

Awareness of own issues, good attention to detail, authoritative, neutral and professional, calm and rational, clear boundaries.

Negotiation

Bottom line clarity, completely focused, composure, clear goals/boundaries, persuasion, leadership, facilitation.

Influencing

Empathy, Goal orientation, Referent use of power, Positive belief, Look right, image, body language, projection, listen, credibility.

Assertiveness

I positive, you positive. Express own needs clearly and concisely Have skills to get needs met without having to win.

Impoverished Skills

Game playing, manipulation, I positive, you negative (or I negative, you positive) choice to learn and move up continuum or'dig in' and become more skilled in impoverished approach.

Next Steps

The Solutions Unlimited Consultancy offers a range of strategies to enhance effectiveness in the work place through executive coaching and more formal development programmes, including the Fast Track to Developing Sophisticated People Skills.

The *People Skills Revolution Skills Companion Workbook* (2012) provides frameworks to enable individuals and groups to explore the issues raised in the book more fully in the context of their own work and personal situations.

For more information or to contact the author visit the Solutions Unlimited website www.Solutionsunlimited.co.uk.